Beyond Discovery

ID0932183

Beyond Discovery

*Moving Academic Research to
the Market*

Jean E. Schelhorn and Joan M. Herbers

OXFORD
UNIVERSITY PRESS

Oxford University Press is a department of the University of Oxford. It furthers
the University's objective of excellence in research, scholarship, and education
by publishing worldwide. Oxford is a registered trade mark of Oxford University
Press in the UK and certain other countries.

Published in the United States of America by Oxford University Press
198 Madison Avenue, New York, NY 10016, United States of America.

© Oxford University Press 2022

All rights reserved. No part of this publication may be reproduced, stored in
a retrieval system, or transmitted, in any form or by any means, without the
prior permission in writing of Oxford University Press, or as expressly permitted
by law, by license, or under terms agreed with the appropriate reproduction
rights organization. Inquiries concerning reproduction outside the scope of the
above should be sent to the Rights Department, Oxford University Press, at the
address above.

You must not circulate this work in any other form
and you must impose this same condition on any acquirer.

Library of Congress Control Number: 2021951290

ISBN 978-0-19-751271-5 (hbk)
ISBN 978-0-19-751270-8 (pbk)

DOI: 10.1093/oso/9780197512715.001.0001

1 3 5 7 9 8 6 4 2

Paperback printed by LSC communications, United States of America
Hardback printed by Bridgeport National Bindery, Inc., United States of America

Contents

Acknowledgments

Our friendship goes back to the 1970s, when we were graduate students at Northwestern University (go Vitamin B's!). We reconnected in 2007 at Ohio State and developed several collaborations there. Most importantly, we came to realize that our complementary backgrounds allow us to offer a new perspective on the discussion about commercialization of academic research.

This book is the product of many years' gestation. Our own experiences are woven throughout, and the result incorporates advice from colleagues, students, mentors, and protégés. We are especially grateful to those who reinforced our conviction that we have something valuable to offer.

We thank those who shared their stories with us, both the triumphs and the disappointments. Watching a researcher catch fire about the potential of their discovery to move into the marketplace is incredibly inspiring, and working with emerging inventors has been a source of great professional satisfaction for us. Similarly, working with the legions of people and organizations that support academic inventors has honed our perspective. We hope that our realistic descriptions increase the odds that you will be the next success story.

We are particularly indebted to Mike Geggenheimer Esq., who freely shared his expertise, time, and words. He was instrumental in helping us sharpen our presentation of intellectual property. In addition, conversations with Mary Albright, Erin Bender, and Michael Mireles clarified key issues. Our experiences as members of X-Squared Angels gave us a behind-the-scenes understanding of how investors think and of common mistakes that start-up companies make in their pitches. Any errors that remain, of course, are our own.

Finally, we thank our families, who provided role models of creativity and inventorship, as well as consistent support and encouragement for anything we wanted to try.

Introduction

You've probably heard a lot about innovation from leaders at your institution; it's certainly in the news a lot. Why? Simply put, innovation fuels the economy. How on earth is that connected to your work as researcher, teacher, mentor, colleague?

Since the 1950s, science and technological innovation has produced more than half of the growth in the United States' Gross Domestic Product,[1] and our future will surely be shaped by innovation as well.[2] The link between scientific/technical innovation and economic growth[3] is promoted in the United States by the Council on Competitiveness,[4] a national consortium of business titans, university leaders, labor leaders, and national laboratory principals. Across the world, entire "ecosystems" that nurture cultures of innovation have developed in places like Silicon Valley in the United States, Zhongguancun in China, and Bangalore in India.

Yet there is a major disconnect: in colleges and universities where much innovation is spawned, academics rarely describe their work as facilitating job creation or economic growth. Higher education is a crucial partner for the competitiveness agenda, but relatively few academic researchers aspire to move their work into the world of commerce. In our experience, they are both intimidated by and uninterested in learning about translating their scholarly work to the marketplace. Leveraging academic innovation to the marketplace remains the exception rather than the rule in most institutions of higher education, and we want to change that.

Beyond Discovery. Jean E. Schelhorn and Joan M. Herbers, Oxford University Press. © Oxford University Press 2022. DOI: 10.1093/oso/9780197512715.001.0001

Why a Book about Commercialization for Academics?

Commercialization is the process of transferring potential and actual intellectual property and related technology/intellectual assets to third parties for use in improving existing products/services or as the basis for new ones. We will deconstruct that definition soon. For now, however, you can think about commercialization as a way to move your discoveries/inventions into the world of selling products and services.

We have worked with many academics who are astounded to learn that their research might have commercial potential; most are intimidated by the strange land known as technology transfer.[5] We believe there is an inventor living inside every academic. After all, discovery is their main goal, and every new discovery has potential for inventive leaps. With coaching, formal programs, and individualized support, many become intrigued by the possibilities of moving their work toward the marketplace. Even so, deep chasms of inexperience and misunderstanding can lead to disenchantment, rookie mistakes, and legal entanglements. With this book, we offer you an overview of the world of academic commercialization, define the roles and responsibilities of various parties that are involved, and offer advice for the journey.

Who Should Read This Book?

We are writing for anyone who has a nascent interest in commercialization and who conducts research in an academic or quasi-academic setting. Thus, faculty, staff, and students in higher education, researchers in federal laboratories, curators in museums—all are potential inventors. We focus on graduate students through faculty researchers, and we cite examples of undergraduate research commercialization along the way.

This book is aimed primarily at research scientists, broadly defined. Our definition of scientist is inclusive, stretching from the social sciences through the natural sciences to applied professional sciences (e.g., health sciences and agriculture) and engineering (collectively called STEM for Science, Technology, Engineering, and Mathematics). We also hope the book proves useful for scholars in other areas, including the arts, humanities, law, and business.

We have policy experts and research administrators in mind as well. Calls for academics to commercialize their research can fall on deaf ears, and messages from those hoping to spur commercialization can be more effective by reframing in ways that address researchers' motivations.[6]

Finally, our discussion stays primarily within the context of systems and laws in the United States, which we know best. Along the way, we describe systems in other countries that are structured differently, and we point out features of the U.S. landscape that can hamper the innovation agenda.[7]

What's in This Book?

In Chapter 1, we lay out the argument for why academic researchers could become interested in commercialization to amplify the impact of their work. Research carried out in laboratories, field locations, and clinics is inspired primarily by *interest*, with a secondary and often compelling motivation to improve the human condition. Yet researchers rarely move directly toward meeting a human need: they write academic papers and give talks to other specialists. We show how commercialization can broaden and deepen the impact of academic research. We also connect experience in commercialization to the shrinking academic job market. Careers outside academia are increasingly attractive, and gaining experience with commercialization is a growing (and advantageous) path for many junior researchers.

Chapter 2 is a tour of the what and how of commercialization. Technology transfer encompasses a variety of legally binding agreements that move inventions out of the institution and into the hands of third parties focused on commercial success. We describe the fundamental elements of those agreements and describe the private-sector entities that seek licenses to institutional assets in order to develop products/services for a market.

Chapter 3 delves into the cultural divide between academic research and commercialization. To be successful in tech transfer, researchers must understand the need to adapt to new mindsets and to learn from others with legal and business experience. We describe key differences between the academic culture and a culture that places primacy on a market-driven mindset. Furthermore, we compare and contrast the skills needed for team-based translation of research to the marketplace. Reward systems are incongruent between the two cultures, and understanding the inherent tension between academic and market-driven value systems is important for researchers and policymakers alike.

Chapter 4 covers intellectual property (IP). Academics used to the free exchange of ideas and results can easily erode their ability to commercialize by failing to understand the legal environment within which protection occurs. The chapter defines IP, describes why IP is important in the marketplace and outlines critical criteria for obtaining IP. We then do a deep dive into patenting. The patenting process is outlined, with associated timelines, and we describe roles of the inventor, tech transfer officers, and patent attorneys. The chapter concludes with a short description of costs to be expected throughout the process.

Chapter 5 describes funding streams available for researchers and how they impose conditions for technology transfer. Institutional (intramural) funds, federal and other grants, and industry-sponsored research have variable conditions for how the results of that funding can and must be commercialized. Finally, we explore the crowdfunding environment, which has emerged as an important source of early support for commercialization.

Chapter 6 provides insider advice grounded in our years of experience working in this domain. It describes common mistakes that impede (and sometimes kill) the possibility of successful commercialization and offers practical advice for the academic inventor. We describe the typical decision processes used in commercialization offices and how researchers can maximize the probability of successfully moving towards the market.

Chapter 7 provides context for an academic who is considering launching a start-up company while still maintaining an academic position. We pose a series of questions to help such individuals explore various roles they might assume in the company, emphasizing differences between academic and start-up cultures. We then describe the rich innovation ecosystem that supports start-ups, including incubators, accelerators, funding agencies, industry, and private capital. We focus on matters specific to academic researchers, referring readers to a wealth of other sources for start-up nuts and bolts.

Chapter 8 treats the uneven playing field in commercialization. Women and non-Asian minority men are severely underrepresented among those who commercialize their research. We document that claim, describe causes for the patterns of underrepresentation, and provide an overview of programs that seek to redress the imbalance.

We wrap up in Chapter 9 with consideration of whether commercialization is right for you. Not every academic is able or willing to engage with technology transfer, although their students might. As in every other human endeavor, practice brings improvement: the second or third invention often is more successful than the first.

The Epilogue offers some thoughts to the administrators and tech transfer officers who are charged with shepherding discoveries/inventions through the various commercialization processes.

Interspersed between our chapters are Profiles that illustrate key points and examples of commercialization arising from academic research. With these Profiles, we aim to help readers visualize their own work moving into the marketplace and to learn from the experiences (both positive and negative) of others.

Finally, we offer a glossary and list of acronyms for quick reference. The notes provide key references and comments that provide additional context.

We want to motivate you to explore how commercialization can amplify the impact of your discoveries. Our book provides a primer on what that means and how it happens, and describes the spectrum of roles you can assume, from mostly spectator to deep involvement in starting and running a company.

So let's get started!

1

Why Should Academic Researchers Consider Commercialization?

Did you know that fluoridated toothpaste, magnetic resonance imaging (MRI) technology, N-95 masks, blood banking, and human contraceptives all have origins in academic research labs? The discoveries that contributed to these successful innovations may well have remained of purely academic interest had not researchers taken active steps to move those discoveries into the realm of invention. By doing so, those inventors changed the world.

You as a researcher want your work to matter. You spend long hours designing, conducting, and analyzing experiments, and then you think hard about how and where to disseminate the results.[1] Researchers present their work via seminars, conference posters and presentations, book chapters, and journal publications—primarily targeting other academic researchers.[2] We now challenge you to think more broadly about taking your messages to additional audiences, especially those that have commercial capabilities.

Our challenge represents our main message to you: by engaging in commercialization, you can multiply the impact of your research. Recall that commercialization is *the process of transferring potential and actual intellectual property and related technology/intellectual assets to third parties[3] for use in improving existing products/services or as the basis for new ones.* The following chapters elaborate on that definition, but first we must position commercialization within the context of how academic researchers work.

Individuals choose academia primarily for the autonomy it promises.[4] Faculty members, especially those in research institutions, can control the hours they work, decide when and

Beyond Discovery. Jean E. Schelhorn and Joan M. Herbers, Oxford University Press. © Oxford University Press 2022. DOI: 10.1093/oso/9780197512715.003.0001

where to publish, and recruit their own students and postdocs; they also have a voice in teaching and service assignments, and they can opt to engage with external organizations such as professional societies.[5] Each scholar has autonomy to choose specific research areas, and for scientists and engineers, problem solving drives the research agenda. Here we mean problem with a lowercase p—the problem is one of personal interest. To be sure, many researchers are also motivated to solve Problems (uppercase P), whether that be curing cancer, improving crop yields, building a better battery, or eliminating pollution. Indeed, when a scientist writes a grant proposal—say, to the National Institutes of Health (NIH) or the Department of Energy (DOE)—such justifications are carefully laid out to position the proposed work within a larger context.[6]

Yet the very nature of research is that Problems must be disassembled into many smaller problems, only a few of which can be pursued in one research group. For example, fundamental to curing some cancers is an understanding of particular immune pathways; improving crop yields may involve tweaking the photosynthetic machinery inside cells; enhancing battery storage can require boosting ion exchange; and reducing water pollution depends on understanding watershed dynamics. Thus, the big Problems identified in grant proposals are parsed into component problems that can be tackled within a funding period.

We want to expand your thinking about how to solve Problems. Perhaps you, like so many academics, have tuned out terms such as *commercialization* or *technology transfer* because they represent a foreign terrain (or maybe a waste of time!). Perhaps you (mistakenly) believe that the only way to commercialize is to start a company. Perhaps you worry about additional demands on your time and attention. Fear not: we will guide you through the terrain, offer options, and show how you can engage the technology transfer enterprise to amplify the reach and impact of your work. Research and commercialization are not incompatible: together they can change the world.

The Academic Mindset

Researchers *do* want their work to matter, but they tend to communicate primarily with each other: they publish in academic journals; they give talks at specialized conferences; they travel to share their work with like-minded researchers. These traditional modes of dissemination are explicitly encoded in the academic reward system, starting at the earliest stages of training. Graduate students may be required to publish before completing their degrees; postdoctoral researchers must have grants, papers, and conference presentations in order to be competitive for a professorial position; and professors themselves are evaluated for raises, tenure, and promotion based in part on those academic credentials. This reward system has metrics for success centered on academic output.[7]

The net result of the traditional academic reward system is that societal impact for most scientific research is a by-product, not the goal, of academic dissemination.[8] In effect, many researchers depend on others to adapt their work for different outlets.[9] They may *write* eloquently about the potential impact of the research on pressing Problems, but most do not *act* to further that agenda.

Academic researchers present two principal arguments for why they do not pursue commercialization. First, many of these researchers believe commercialization is antithetic to the academic ideals of free and open exchange. This belief is misguided, however. To be beneficial, any discovery must ultimately become used or adopted widely, which does not happen by accident: adoption of academic results requires that they be translated to a product or service valuable in the marketplace. Translation in turn requires that a third party becomes interested in developing the research discovery for the market, thereby making a profit. The ideals of free and open exchange may yield products/services in the public domain, but they rarely offer an advantage that produces market success. Thus, traditional academic dissemination without concurrent efforts to commercialize is extremely unlikely to solve the Problems that motivate researchers.

A second frequently-voiced argument is that any results developed from public funding by definition belong to the public. Not only does this mindset ignore the power of the marketplace to change the world, but it betrays ignorance of a fundamental reality: many researchers are *obligated* as a condition of their funding and/or employment to disclose inventions. We explain this point fully in Chapter 5 and provide best practices for how to meet those obligations in Chapter 6.[10]

Our core argument, then, is that the big Problems that motivate academic researchers can best be solved if market-oriented[11] partners become involved. Cancer drugs must be approved for use, manufactured, and marketed; clean energy technology must be optimized, fine-tuned in field trials, and then mass-produced. Those processes are the realm of business, not academia.

Indeed, many businesses rely on innovation that starts in academic labs. Science and engineering industries exploit the tendency of academic researchers to freely share their research and those companies have an infrastructure to scout for novel approaches originating in university labs. Industry scientists scour the academic literature and attend scientific meetings to identify innovations related to their core businesses. Many identify "thought leaders" who freely contribute ideas to industry[12] and can then develop those ideas for the marketplace. Some companies enter into explicit partnerships[13] with universities for developing products/services with market potential. As industry has cut back on its own research and development, it has increasingly mined academic research—exploiting the fact that academics freely share their work.[14]

How Can Commercialization Fit into the Academic Culture?

Small wonder that institutions find it difficult to interest faculty in commercialization, which academics view as a foreign enterprise.[15] In our experience, many researchers are frustrated that their work has not realized its potential for solving Problems, but they cannot envision a reasonable pathway toward that end. While researchers would like their work to interest external entities, their passivity reflects three main challenges: they have limited time, insufficient knowledge of the terrain, and no institutional incentive to engage in commercialization.[16]

We believe the primary incentive for researchers to commercialize is the ability of commercialization to help solve Problems with a capital P. Using that frame, faculty understand that partnering with outside entities can leverage their research in ways that academic dissemination never will. The primary hook by which institutions can encourage researchers to engage with commercialization is its link to societal impact.[17] Because every researcher wants their work to matter, emphasizing how commercialization can amplify impact becomes a powerful motivator.[18]

Academic institutions would do well to look to other research organizations that embed technology transfer within their cultures.[19] In particular, federal laboratories have a mission to provide services and products for their core constituents, many of whom are in the private sector. To fulfill that mission, federal labs not only recognize commercialization within their rewards structure but actively encourage it with infrastructures that emphasize training for researchers, provide well-staffed tech transfer offices, and highlight successes.[20] These institutions can point to myriad products and services we use every day.[21] The Federal Laboratory Consortium[22] highlights those successes and shares best practices for furthering the commercialization agenda.

In the next few chapters, we explore the commercialization terrain and help you define your goals. It is important to understand that tech transfer is a team sport and that you as an academic inventor are just one member of the team. Teammates include collaborators, students, professional staff in tech transfer, administrators, likeminded colleagues, industry contacts, and others. As a team member, you can sit on the bench most of the time, or you can be deeply involved. We have worked with academic inventors across that spectrum. Some report their inventions and then trust the tech transfer office to take further actions while they return to their research programs; others actively support the commercialization agenda by developing solid partnerships with that office; and still others start companies to move the technology toward the market. There are multiple pathways to successful commercialization, any of which can produce lasting impact.

Early-Career Academics

Graduate students and postdoctoral fellows are the engines of most academic research: their hands titrate, plant, build, and code. Furthermore, their ideas help shape research agendas for the lab director (known in academia as the Principal Investigator, or PI). For the most part, the training of graduate students and postdocs is decentralized and based on an apprentice model. In science and engineering, graduate students and postdocs are most often paid from grants and contracts awarded to the institution on behalf of the PI.[23] Thus, their primary responsibility is to that PI's research agenda.

The PI is steeped in academic culture, and most train their students primarily to excel at academic research. Yet, those trainees face a terribly uncertain job market. Academic jobs are scarce and highly competitive, while industry jobs are affected by economic factors and may bring little job security. The biomedical sciences have overproduced research students for decades,[24] and even in some engineering disciplines, the market for PhD-trained scientists is highly competitive. Not surprisingly, graduate students and postdocs become increasingly disenchanted with the academic enterprise.[25] A landmark study[26] documented that career ambitions of graduate students within the prestigious University of California system flipped from early interest in academic careers to prevailing disinterest by the time of degree completion. Clearly, PIs who think they are training tomorrow's professors are deluded.

Not surprisingly, research trainees who face shifting employment prospects are eager to learn about nonacademic options, including the world of commercialization.[27] However, if the PI is not interested in commercialization, student researchers may be discouraged from even thinking about translation to the marketplace. Worse still, if trainees do not understand the fundamental rules of public disclosure (see Chapter 6), a push to publish could obliterate the opportunity to commercialize[28] that many of them desire.

We believe that graduate programs, especially in science and engineering, should include options for training in commercialization,[29] with appropriate messaging of encouragement from their supervisors.[30] A PI who does not (or will not) find the time to interface with the tech transfer office can be persuaded to allow a graduate student or postdoc to do so. Not only do many trainee scientists want to explore careers other than academia, but they can be very effective conduits for commercialization of a lab's discoveries.[31] Indeed, start-up companies often employ the junior scientists whose discoveries are being developed for commercial markets, and early-stage academics can have traits and values that engender success, as we explore in Chapter 3.[32] We are optimistic that the coming generations of researchers will be more open to commercialization.[33]

A Note on Terminology

We have used various words to describe the outputs of academic research (collectively known as intellectual assets, as we describe more fully in the next chapter), and now we must distinguish nuances of meaning. A *discovery* is a new-to-the-world insight/finding/understanding arising from the research process. Within those insights/findings, one might have an *invention* that has a legal definition: first, it must be new (first-in-the-world), nonobvious, and it must have a use; next it must fall within special legally defined categories: composition of matter, method/process, device/article, or plant. The invention that meets these criteria and categories can form the basis for filing for a patent (covered in Chapter 4). Inventions are typically deployed for practical purposes in combination with other know-how or elements as *technologies*. The application of technologies to needs that may be known (pull) or unknown (push) in society is sometimes referred to as *innovation*, especially when the impact is large.

Conclusion

We contend that commercialization enhances the potential impact of research discoveries for the societal good. We want to demystify this territory for you, whether you are a student or a professor, and we want to help you make good choices about moving research outputs into the world of business. Then perhaps you can truly solve capital-P Problems!

PROFILE: Patrick Brown

In 2009, Pat Brown was a highly successful biochemist with a prestigious job at Stanford University and membership in the National Academy of Sciences. Beyond traditional career accomplishments such as grants and publications, Brown also co-founded the Public Library of Science (PLOS) and invented the DNA microarray, which is now a cornerstone of research and diagnostic labs.

He also was keenly interested in using his talents to solve pressing social problems.[1] Brown took a sabbatical in 2009 and decided to tackle the globally significant problem of how livestock production contributes to greenhouse gas emissions and environmental degradation. He studied the industry as well as the qualities of meat that consumers value, and he decided to develop products that would provide the taste and nutritional profile of meat, relying on plant products rather than growing livestock. Global meat sales represent a $1.2 trillion market, which persuaded venture capitalists to invest in his company (and him) at a very early stage.

At age 60, Brown retired from his academic position and in 2011 he founded Impossible Foods, Inc. He hired a CEO with business experience and several scientists to work on product development. Brown had a key insight: what people enjoy about meat is the taste, texture, and sensory experiences that arise from molecules containing heme. Heme is an iron-containing compound essential for life and is ubiquitous in living organisms. His team set out to harvest heme first from soybean roots and then yeast, and use it as a component to build a product that looks, smells, and tastes like beef. The company experimented with ingredients and recipes until they had such a product.

Beyond Discovery. Jean E. Schelhorn and Joan M. Herbers, Oxford University Press. © Oxford University Press 2022. DOI: 10.1093/oso/9780197512715.003.0002

The Impossible™ Burger launched in 2016, having secured Food and Drug Administration (FDA) approval. Brown won the endorsement of celebrity chefs and pundits alike, and restaurants nationwide offered his products. Impossible™ products have since been adopted by fast-food chains, including White Castle and Burger King; Little Caesar's offers pizzas with Impossible™ sausage, and Starbucks has its Impossible™ Breakfast Sandwich. The Impossible™ Burger appeared in stores in 2019 and is stocked by national grocers, including Kroger.[2]

The company is currently valued at $4B, and it has raised about $1.2B in venture capital. While Brown received an exit offer several years ago from Google, he declined to sell his company because he was deeply invested in the mission of offering plant-based meat to customers. The company's main focus now is scaling up; while it sells "tens of millions" of pounds of product today, Brown intends to ramp up production by orders of magnitude in the coming years. Impossible Foods, Inc. also continues to work on new products and hopes to offer steak in the near future.

And it certainly appears that Brown knows a bit about intellectual property: there are 20 U.S.-issued patents assigned to Impossible Foods, Inc.,[3] along with a host of related international filings. He has also used trademark protection vigorously and doubtless has trade secrets tucked away as well that secure the value proposition.

2

Commercialization and How It Happens

The world of commercialization has its own vocabulary, mindset, and criteria that few academic researchers understand without experience. In this chapter, we demystify commercialization so you can learn how it works.

Let's start with what you do best: create and disseminate knowledge. These are academic institutions' core missions. Knowledge creation is the domain of academic research, whether it occurs in a laboratory, field site, collaborator's institution, or library. Academics disseminate knowledge through their teaching programs, publication/presentations, and outreach/engagement. Indeed, most of the knowledge transfer from the institution to the external world occurs via their students' lifelong contributions to society. Here we hope to broaden your ideas about dissemination and engagement to include additional internal and external partners who focus on commercialization.

Sometimes research leads to a discovery/insight/invention/technology that could be pivotal in solving an unmet societal need. You may not even realize its possible applications or uses for some years! Once you start thinking about how your discovery might improve the current state, the ball is in your court to decide how you want to proceed with communicating your findings and insights. Of course, you need to publish your work and give talks to colleagues, which will help you to better understand its significance and possibilities for the marketplace. We also strongly suggest that you engage with commercialization professionals early in that process. They can collaborate with you to provide new perspectives on how your work

Beyond Discovery. Jean E. Schelhorn and Joan M. Herbers, Oxford University Press. © Oxford University Press 2022. DOI: 10.1093/oso/9780197512715.003.0003

could translate eventually to the marketplace, perspectives that can shape future career decisions.

Recall our definition: commercialization is the process of transferring potential and actual intellectual property and related technology/intellectual assets to third parties for use in improving existing products/services or as the basis for new ones. Commercialization offices play critical roles in moving researcher insights and resultant inventions/technology through processes that might lead to another party taking the commercial lead. That goal can be achieved in various ways: commercialization is rarely a linear process, nor is it often simple.[1] However, by learning the basics of how technology transfer happens, you can gain confidence to take steps that might move your discoveries into products of interest to external partners. Much of the heavy lifting in academic commercialization is done by others, and we point out the times at which you play crucial roles. Indeed, you might yourself become the commercial partner if you decide to start a company. We have more to say on that subject in Chapter 7.

We explore the chasm between traditional academic culture and technology transfer in the next chapter. Here we focus on the actual mechanics of how "your technology" (which almost certainly does not belong to you, as we explain in Chapter 5) can move through internal assessments and processes and perhaps be positioned to move out of your institution into the hands of teams that want to translate the work to the marketplace. This chapter creates a common context for subsequent chapters that provide further critical information, best practices, and specific steps for you as the inventor in this process. We also introduce some important vocabulary that you must begin to understand.[2]

While on the subject of vocabulary, let us be clear about two terms: intellectual assets and intellectual property (IP).[3] We use the term *intellectual assets* to denote know-how and its codifications. Know-how refers to the totality of expertise and skills needed to solve a problem or carry out a procedure.[4] That know-how is codified in academic products, including written methods, materials, data, software, hardware, firmware, other writings, recorded communications, and various kinds of creative output (e.g., works of art, music, scripts). Faculty, staff, and students alike generate intellectual assets through their work, some of which may be appropriate for commercialization. Some intellectual assets can become *intellectual property* through legally defined processes (e.g., patents, trademarks, and copyrights), subject to strict criteria; we define IP and cover it more fully in Chapter 4. Note that a patent by itself does not constitute commercialization but may serve to facilitate it. Conversely, numerous routes to commercialization can occur without a patent. Patenting and commercialization are related, to be sure, but are not mutually inclusive.

For universities and other entities like federal labs, there are very limited direct paths to markets: tax laws allow nonprofits to offer products/services only in specific categories (medical services, education services, animal rescue, arts delivery, etc.)[5] or via earnings units (e.g., university hospitals) or affiliated entities in approved categories. Beyond those categories, nonprofit entities by and large can only translate their discoveries/insights/technologies into the market through the efforts of third parties. Technology transfer puts assets in the hands of external teams that are not constrained in terms of commercialization.

Who Does What?

Your primary role is to ensure that your institutionally supported research[6] is conducted with excellence and, when possible, supports the case for novelty.[7] With something novel in hand, you may be interested in enlisting the advice and support of commercialization professionals in your institution and region that are charged with moving intellectual assets toward the market. Most medium-to-large academic institutions have one or more offices staffed with individuals who know how to navigate the commercialization landscape.[8] Often called technology transfer or commercialization, these offices and staff may be centralized, embedded within academic units, or situated in a separate organization altogether. Furthermore, some consortia have their own operations.[9] So your first step is to investigate how commercialization support is structured locally; Box 2.1 describes the prototype of tech transfer, at the University of Wisconsin.

Wherever it resides and however configured, technology transfer units have formal authority to translate institution-owned intellectual assets to external entities, as dictated by policy. Let us be clear about these assets: you as a researcher develop them, but in most cases the institution owns them as a condition of your employment and as stipulated in institutional policy. We return to the topic of ownership in Chapter 5.

The scope of activities for commercialization offices include training for researchers; intake and assessment of research insights/inventions/creations; electing title and complying with other requirements for U.S. federally funded inventions that the institution

---

Box 2.1 The beginnings of technology transfer

The origins of tech transfer can be traced to Madison, Wisconsin. In the early 1920s, University of Wisconsin (UW) biochemist Harry Steenbock discovered that exposure to ultraviolet light allowed some fats to absorb Vitamin D. This discovery had immense potential for human health, and Steenbock wished to patent it, with any potential revenue going to UW. Because no mechanism to handle patents and licensing existed then, the university in 1925 established the Wisconsin Alumni Research Foundation (WARF), a separate nonprofit corporation to be run by alumni. WARF's first commercial success was built on Steenbock's discovery, a means to incorporate Vitamin D in dairy products to prevent the bone disease rickets. Since then, WARF has patented thousands of innovations (nearly 200 patents issued in 2019 alone) and funneled millions of dollars into UW research labs. Noteworthy inventions include warfarin, an anticlotting agent, MRI imaging technology, and computer chip innovations. In 2003, WARF was awarded the National Medal of Technology and Innovation by President George W. Bush.

seeks to commercialize; IP development and protection; marketing of potential and actual IP assets; and negotiation, execution, and management of a suite of legally binding agreements.[10] In some cases, the tech transfer office is responsible for negotiating industry-sponsored research agreements as well, and it typically interfaces with industry partnership teams, venture development teams, and local or regional economic development efforts.

These are service offices, and their personnel want to help you! They guide navigation of the commercialization options we summarize below, and we describe their roles throughout the rest of the book. As professionals, many belong to the Association of University Technology Managers (AUTM) and/or the Licensing Executive Society (LES); these associations share best practices, updates on regulatory and legal matters, and data on many of the topics we cover in this book.

You may be surprised to learn that some of their activities, such as negotiating and executing Material Transfer Agreements (MTAs), do not seem like "commercialization." We will show how involving this office in aspects of collaboration with extrainstitutional entities (other universities, federal labs, nonprofits, industry) provides important guidance and in some cases protection for your work.

How Commercialization Happens

For commercialization to proceed from a nonprofit institution, rights to the IP and associated intellectual assets owned by the institution must be transferred from the nonprofit to an entity or individual focused on commercial activity. The transfer occurs through various types of legally binding agreements.[11] The agreements permit the party or entity to move forward to develop and sell products/services with the technology of interest as a component in, or as the entire basis for, commercial products/services. The institution typically retains ownership of the transferred assets, as well as the ability to continue research, educational, and outreach activities with those assets. That is, establishing commercialization agreements for the technology does not restrict your ability to use it within the academic context, but rather allows commercialization activities to be led and undertaken by others.

Many types/categories of agreements are used to promote commercialization, which requires negotiation to reach terms acceptable to all parties. All such agreements share three pivotal sections that you must understand: (1) the grant of rights; (2) the licensed use; and (3) the term of the grant of rights.

The *grant of rights* section and associated schedules/exhibits detail what the interested purchaser (licensee) is obtaining from the seller (licensor and owner of the asset(s)). The grant of rights, or grant, is the WHAT that is being transferred to the licensee through the agreement. The grant can be exclusive or nonexclusive. If nonexclusive, the licensor can offer the same grant to additional entities.[12] Again, rights to use the asset for research and education are typically reserved by the licensing institution.

The *use* or *licensed field* of the grant is the WHY the grant of rights is being sought and being made. Use can be restricted, for example to commercial use in a single field; or at the extreme the use can be all uses, in all fields (e.g., areas of use or applications). Uses can be for research only (option agreements, described below); evaluation, research, and testing toward commercial ends; or commercial purposes as defined in the agreement. The licensee requests a use/field or uses/fields in the negotiation steps of the agreement, and it is up to the licensor to agree or to restrict the use if deemed appropriate. There can be multiple (nonexclusive) licenses on a given technology, or there can be one exclusive license. Clearly, assessment of the requested use is an important consideration. The use also has an associated territory; most academic licenses grant worldwide uses.[13]

The *term* of the agreement establishes HOW LONG the grant is in effect.[14] If the grant is to pending or issued patents, the term is typically the life of the patent application(s) and issued patent(s) and all patents that can be derived from the original patent filings. At the time of this writing, the term of a U.S. utility patent is 20 years from the date of first filing; design patents have a term of 15 years from the date the design patent is granted.[15] If the agreement is a data or material transfer agreement not linked to a license agreement,[16] the term can be as short as six months to one year.

Common agreements that confer a grant of rights include option and license agreements; data or material transfer agreements; plant variety agreements; permissions; Cooperative Research and Development Agreements (CRADAs, used at U.S. federal labs); copyright and/or trademark agreements; distribution agreements; and agreements configured for special circumstances.[17] The rest of this chapter focuses on option and license agreements.

An *option agreement* is often a first step. This type of agreement allows an interested party or entity to fully evaluate the strength and breadth of a technology or technology platform. It can allow that party (the optionee) to perform research and/or develop a business plan for the use that captures estimates of the development costs, timelines, required funding amounts/sources, market analysis, and projections of sales revenues that might result.[18] The optionee may need to assure themselves that there is a real market need that the technology can address, or address in conjunction with other technology, and that the market size is sufficient to warrant their focus and business efforts on obtaining funding at the levels required for success. During the term, the optionee likely also assesses the patentability of any patent applications detailed in the grant of rights[19] and may begin to assess any possible IP complications that may surface in the intended fields of use. Such reviews often are conducted by intellectual property lawyers working on behalf of the optionee. The optionee may also pursue funding, such as grants or investments, to support product development.

The option period provides time to assess interest in pursuing a commercial license and confers a right to "exercise the option" at any time during the option period; exercising the option triggers negotiation of a license agreement.[20] In short, the optionee uses the option agreement to decide if it wants to move into a license agreement.[21] During the option period, the optionee has three alternatives: (1) they may walk away; (2) they may seek to renew the option agreement; or (3) they may exercise the option to negotiate a license agreement. In some instances, the optionee may require that critical terms of any future license agreement be negotiated and appended to the option agreement (often referred to as a license term sheet). Developing and appending a term sheet can lengthen the timeline to negotiate the option agreement but may reduce the timeline for negotiation of a final license agreement should the option be exercised.

Option agreements are easy to negotiate compared with license agreements and place relatively few financial obligations on the optionee. The term can be as short as a few months or as long as one year, and option agreements are typically renewable with mutual consent at least one time. Option agreements likely require a payment from the optionee in exchange for the grant of rights, optioned use/field/territory, and the term of the option. This can be a stand-alone up-front fee, or payment can be applicable to a future license fee. Other financial requirements in option agreements typically include payment of all patent costs incurred by the licensor during the term of the option agreement.[22]

Typically, the licensor supplies an agreement template for consideration by the optionee.[23] Thereafter multiple steps of negotiation can occur, adding requirements sought by the optionee or the licensor and those additions receiving consideration by the parties. A back-and-forth discussion occurs, with multiple red-line versions exchanged before the parties reach terms. The agreement then moves to execution, requiring formal signature. For both parties there is a signatory with authority to sign the final agreement. In academic settings, this authority rarely resides with colleges, departments, or individual faculty. Rather, higher-level administrators with authority to bind the institution sign after legal, conflict, and other final reviews are completed. Typically, these negotiations are opaque for researchers, who often do not even see the business terms in the agreements that are executed on assets they have conceived or developed.

The technology is "locked-up" during the option period, and there is no guarantee that a license will result. Termination of such agreements is far easier for the optionee than the licensor. The option agreement may only specify that the optionee has to give notice of termination (such as 30 days); the agreement can also specify that the optionee must share any results obtained during the option period. For the licensor, however, there are very few paths to terminate an option agreement prior to expiration of the option term. Further, if the optionee exercises its option, the institution must proceed in good faith toward a license. If the parties fail to reach terms for a license within the stipulated negotiation period, the licensee has no further obligations to the former optionee, and the technology is no longer encumbered.[24]

A *license agreement* can be a first or second step (following an option agreement). The license agreement includes the three topics discussed above, and it also conveys the right to commercialize products/services utilizing the licensed technology. At least two additional critical topics are negotiated/finalized: financial consideration concerning what and when (and in some cases how) the licensee will pay the licensor, and milestones required to advance the technology. Many additional sections/topics and conditions add complexity, which is warranted because a license agreement binds the parties for commercial translation and may be in force for many years.[25] By granting a license, the institution is placing confidence in the licensee to commercially deploy the institutional asset(s) and to share some level of the value that is created through binding financial terms. Again, back-and-forth negotiations between parties ensue until (with persistence) an agreement can be reached.

In addition to time-based milestones linked to a development plan and associated fee schedule, a license agreement typically includes consideration such as up-front fees, annual maintenance fees, historic and future patent costs, and royalty payments that return a percentage of revenue from future sales to the licensor. The royalty percentage varies by maturity of technology, development path, breadth of patent portfolio, and intended use. This negotiation can get complicated! For example, royalty stacking may be addressed. Should multiple licenses be required for the licensee to develop a product for the market, the licensee may seek to limit or cap the royalties that come due. There may be other conditions (for example, sublicensing). For start-up or new companies, equity[26] also factors into the financial consideration. There may be a parallel sponsored research agreement that funnels money to the academic laboratory for additional research and development to advance the technology. Each negotiation is unique!

If your invention attracts a licensee, you may in time receive revenue into your pocket or to your laboratory. Every institution has its own algorithm for distributing license/royalty revenue to institutional coffers, inventors/creators, the commercialization office itself, the college, the department, and the researcher's lab. Those amounts and how they are credited to you can take the form of additions to your paycheck or deposits in a discretionary account under your control.[27] Note that many license agreements stipulate that prior costs borne by the institution (e.g., for patent preparation and prosecution) must first be defrayed. There are examples of blockbuster licenses that generate considerable returns (see Box 2.2), and perhaps you can land one for your institution.

License agreements usually provide the ability to sublicense or transfer commercialization rights to another party. That is, a licensee may obtain a binding license, and in time those rights may be transferred to a third party through sublicense terms. For example, an early-stage licensee may lack the ability to scale the ultimate product into all markets and may engage a sublicensee for certain market offerings.[28] This can be a surprise to the inventor/creator but is not uncommon, and typically it indicates commercial progress. Such a sublicense arrangement may also be within the original business plan of the licensee.

In these negotiations there are few absolutes, and the process should be viewed as an active discussion/negotiation between

---

Box 2.2 A blockbuster drug license

The most lucrative academic license to date belongs to Northwestern University, which licensed a compound created in Richard Silverman's lab that became the pain medication Lyrica®. The university has realized $1.4B and counting from this one license.

willing partners, one seeking to transfer the technology to another party, and one wanting to incorporate the technology into products and services that can be sold in the future at a profit. The license must provide the licensee sufficient rights to be successful and investable (financial terms that are acceptable to investors if the business plan requires such investment). Typically, the term of the license reflects the enforcement term of any IP (and its derivatives) provided through the grant. In some cases, the term of the agreement can be established as a point of negotiation, or it can be "evergreen" or "perpetual."[29]

Successful licensees move the technology forward, reporting back to the institution as required in the agreement. On the other hand, if the licensee is unsuccessful getting to market, the assets still remain in the licensee's hands as long as they meet requirements in the license agreement. As was the case for option agreements, license agreements are easy for the licensee to terminate. Typically, they require a 30–60-day notification of termination, and compliance with the other license terms up through the date of termination such as authorized and incurred costs and possibly other information exchange. For the licensor, however, termination usually requires a material breach of the agreement that was not corrected during the time period specified for correction. Licenses are indeed terminated, and the technology can be re-licensed; time, however, cannot be recovered as markets shift and IP protection clocks tick.

To summarize, these legally binding agreements provide a grant of rights to the receiving party for the technology and associated IP or possibly related assets, for a specific use or field, and for a given time period. They spell out financial consideration due to the licensor in exchange for the grant of rights provided to the licensee, as well as a host of other conditions that the parties require. Negotiations can be protracted, as many issues are discussed and internal reviews are conducted by each party; the researcher is left out of most negotiations.[30] Through these steps, the technology moves along a path for commercialization, which can culminate in improvements to existing products or services or new products and services introduced in the marketplace.

Who/What Is Interested in Licensing?

The preceding discussion describes how technology is transferred to other parties via legally binding agreements: that is what tech transfer means. The commercialization office is charged with marketing those technologies to various external parties; they do so by developing advertising materials that outline the *value proposition* of the technology (much more on value propositions in Chapter 7!) and disseminating those materials widely to their networks. Many companies actively review your institution's websites that contain these materials, and some may approach you, the researcher, or your office to learn more. Should that initial display of interest get serious, negotiations can begin.

What kinds of entities sit across the table to negotiate? Most often, the potential licensee is a for-profit business.[31] In rare cases, an individual seeks to option/license, or a not-for-profit becomes interested in a technology. We focus here on for-profit business licensees.

We distinguish between established companies and new/relatively new companies. Established large companies seeking licenses typically agree to a number of financial terms (payments as percent of net sales, e.g., royalties; milestone plans and payments; up-front license fees; patent costs) but rarely, if ever, offer equity. New/relatively new companies are called start-up companies, newcos (shorthand for new company), or spin-outs,[32] and they usually offer (or may be required to offer) equity in addition to other consideration as part of the license agreement. In its 2018 report[33] gleaned from member institution self-reported data, AUTM indicated that, of technologies that were licensed, 23% went to large companies, 18% to start-ups, and 59% to other small companies.

Should your technology not attract a license, at some point the commercialization office is unlikely to entertain further interest. Depending on institutional policy, you may be able to license the technology yourself. If you decide to pursue that option, you should only do so with eyes and ears wide open, as we explore in Chapter 7.

Conclusion

Technology transfer is by definition transfer of technology out of the institution and into another entity. That entity seeks to make and ultimately sell a product or offer a service that incorporates the transferred technology. The commercialization office is your partner in this quest, and they engage in myriad activities toward that end. All tech transfer occurs via legally binding agreements, which can take various forms and for which your role may be limited.[34] Even so, knowing the basics will help you understand the process as well as give you insight into how a particular path emerges. Next, we explore how the world of commercialization compares and contrasts with academic culture. A deep understanding of that topic will make you a more engaged and helpful partner in the commercialization process.

Profile: Peter Tsai

Peter Tsai is a materials scientist who has conducted extensive research on nonwoven materials, especially melt-blown fibers and webs. He helped solve many important unmet needs, especially for filtration improvement, and his inventions/patents have been commercially significant for many industrial and medical applications.

Taiwanese-born Tsai came to the United States after graduating college and working at the Taiwan Textile Research Institute. He received his PhD in materials science from Kansas State University in 1984, and then he accepted a position at the University of Tennessee, where he remained until his retirement in 2019 and is now an Emeritus Professor.

A major focus of Tsai's research has been improving materials for use in filtering substances out of the air and also improving the wettability of web/nonwoven materials. His patented inventions span methods for manufacturing as well as creating articles. An especially important innovation uses electrostatic charging of the web or composite structures, leading to enhanced properties for nonwoven layers or articles. These approaches improve the filtering/capture capability of those materials by orders of magnitude. One such category of filtered particles comprises pathogens (like viruses—to be specific, SARS-Cov-2).

While Tsai's technology has been incorporated into numerous filtration products for home and industry, protection of humans themselves with the N95 mask is perhaps the most recognizable. These masks, used in construction and hospitals alike, contribute to human health by filtering out very small particles: the N means "not resistant to oil" (focused on industrial protection needs) while the

Beyond Discovery. Jean E. Schelhorn and Joan M. Herbers, Oxford University Press. © Oxford University Press 2022. DOI: 10.1093/oso/9780197512715.003.0004

95 refers to its ability to filter out 95% of particles that are smaller than a micron—including bacteria and viruses. Today the N95 mask is our gold standard for respirators and is in high demand: more than a billion people worldwide had benefited from its use *prior to the pandemic*. As the COVID-19 pandemic surged, the "N95 mask" became a household phrase with health systems, construction workers, and consumers like you and me wanting to exploit its filtration capabilities simply to breathe safely. The severe shortage of these masks brought Tsai out of retirement to offer his expertise to the world.

The N95 mask is an example of an academic innovation contributing to solving an enormous societal problem, but Tsai's contributions do not stop there. His innovations have contributed to numerous other products: he is a named inventor on 12 issued patents, and his inventions are the basis for 20 commercial licenses. He has consulted for 170+ companies, trained legions of students in his laboratory, and been honored with numerous awards. We can all breathe easier, thanks to you, Peter Tsai!

3

Adapting to the World
of Commercialization

"We are rightfully proud of our growing leadership at the
frontiers of research, but we should also play a leading role
in translating that knowledge into use"

— Patrick Gallagher[1]

Now that you have a basic understanding of how commercialization
works, we turn to shifts in mindset and behaviors that will make you
a more effective partner in translational efforts. Knowing how commercialization happens is just the first step: you also must adapt to a
different culture.

You have trained in research-oriented environments, whether
they be universities, government laboratories, or institutes. In these
environments, you learned what to expect from interactions with
academic colleagues, how to communicate with them, and what the
standards of excellence are. To excel in commercialization, you need
to engage partners beyond your peers. For success, you will need
to become comfortable with a different, yet complementary, set of
values and commit to learn from and collaborate with professional
colleagues who have content knowledge outside your expertise.
Quite probably new skills, behaviors, and actions must be acquired,
and certainly you must learn new vocabulary.[2] So, let us explore
options for researchers to reframe their thinking and identify traits
crucial to success in the new environment of commercialization.[3]

Beyond Discovery. Jean E. Schelhorn and Joan M. Herbers, Oxford University Press. © Oxford University Press
2022. DOI: 10.1093/oso/9780197512715.003.0005

The journey starts with results stemming from your research program. Two considerations take priority. First, has your research yielded insights or discoveries that are substantially new? To be sure, all research adds to our body of knowledge. Sometimes, though, you may have a breakthrough in understanding or unexpected results that represent a new and important discovery. This should prompt you to consider options for follow-up translational research or even steps toward commercialization. Just as the significance of your findings drives a cascade of academic decisions, including how and where to apply for funding, where to submit manuscripts for publication, and the like, so too does significance affect commercialization decisions. Incremental results are rarely published in top-tier journals, nor do they tend to elicit interest from potential commercialization partners; it is the game-changing discoveries that attract attention from your academic colleagues and that also have potential to offer solutions to unmet needs that exist in the market.

Culture Shift: Reframe Problems as Unmet Needs

In Chapter 1 we described how researchers wish to solve problems. We now shift our attention to reframing those problems as unmet need(s). This reframing prompts a series of questions for commercialization:

- Is there a direct connection between your results and a specific identified need?
- Have you invented something that will allow people to do something that is currently impossible or difficult to do?
- Do your innovations address any "pain points," and how sure are you that the pain points are real?

This concept of unmet need is easy for academics to grasp. The next step is to tweak the concept toward commercialization: identifying a significant (large and potentially profitable) unmet need *in the marketplace*. Success in commercialization requires not only innovation, but also connection to an unmet need for which a market exists or could be developed.

Results that prove significant for commercialization come from three modes of innovation: *technology push* (technical results-centric), *market pull* (users-centric), or *societal challenges* (world and humanity centric).[4]

Technology push occurs if a discovery may have market potential, but the need may not be recognized. In essence, such a discovery must ultimately be pushed into the marketplace, but the pathway to market is not clear. Innovators can seek help from "imagineers"[5] who identify potential new, or perhaps existing, applications where the discovery might competitive advantage. Should a possible fit between the innovation and a market be identified, then champions with the requisite talent/business skills are needed to move forward.[6]

Does any of the above sound like typical activities in academia? Most academic researchers are poorly equipped to strategize about potential markets, but must rely on others, perhaps staff in the tech transfer office or perhaps a licensee. Push innovation can take years to become commercially viable: for example, lasers were of primarily academic interest for decades until they were incorporated into applications such as fiber-optic technology and surgery.

Stories of push innovation abound in books and articles about scientific serendipity.[7] These stories rarely speak to the nature of the path to market in the terminology we just introduced. Microwave oven technology started when an engineer noticed his candy bar melted when he stood near a magnetron vacuum tube; the accidental production of corn flakes revolutionized the breakfast foods market; a failed adhesive applied to a notepaper to become the Post-it* provided an entirely new functionality for paper that had immediate appeal in the market. In short, discoveries can include errors or unintended experiments that are then pushed into the market.

Market pull innovation occurs when researchers specifically seek new solutions for existing needs/shortcomings for offerings in the market, or find that their discovery does so. These innovations can stem from serendipity, with perhaps the most famous example being penicillin: the accidental discovery that fungi produced a substance that killed bacteria in itself pointed to the existing unmet need for infection control.

Virtually all applied research is pull innovation.[8] Indeed, many units within universities have a mandate to conduct applied research (e.g., agriculture, clinical medicine),[9] and some disciplines encourage industrial partnerships (via CRADAs in federal laboratories and industry-sponsored research in universities).

Sometimes the invent-to-need pull comes from *societal challenges*, leading to the third class of innovation, which is best exemplified by the current COVID-19 pandemic that has generated many invent-to-need innovations. Needs for personal protective equipment (PPE), retrofitted equipment, diagnostics, vaccines, therapeutics, treatment protocols—all provoked researchers, government laboratories, and companies[10] to look for solutions. The pandemic induced radical shifts in personal behavior, business methods, regulatory processes—and tech transfer. New partnerships were forged, and federal funding programs were streamlined to rapidly recruit, evaluate, and fund proposals that showed promise. Citizen science initiatives like Folding@Home[11] pivoted toward the need to understand the novel coronavirus. Similarly, societal needs for online-everything prompted huge shifts in technology needs and potential solutions. Figuring out distribution channels for administering vaccines has created new partnerships between government and industry as well.

To facilitate tech transfer for these innovations, a consortium of business and universities developed the Open Covid Pledge[12] to "make intellectual property available free of charge" for meeting the emergency. Similarly, three universities established the COVID-19 Technology Access Framework[13] to accelerate licensing for related technologies. The Association of University Technology Managers (AUTM) issued licensing guidelines for COVID-19 innovations, as did groups across the globe. In addition, the United States Patent and Trademark Office (USPTO) offered streamlined reviews and reduced fees for IP related to COVID-19.[14]

Emergencies drive invent-to-need and pull innovation. The behavior of academic researchers during such crises illustrates our contention that they engage in commercialization primarily for the sake of societal impact.

Finally, some innovations are so striking that they create new markets. Visionaries like Steve Jobs and the founders of AirBNB were able to develop entirely new technologies, products, and services that became instant must-haves. People did not even know they wanted an iPod or a short-term apartment rental until they became available. Such disruptive innovation does occur in research labs[15] and often leads the researcher into a new career, as our profile of Patrick Brown illustrates.

Culture Shift: It's All about the Market

Identifying an unmet need is an important step. Most researchers are enthralled with their inventions/discoveries and believe others will readily grasp their importance. Yet academics passionate about their discoveries may not have any context for market realities. Many an academic has been bitterly disappointed when they come to understand how small the market is (Box 3.1).

Box 3.1 Market size matters

A clinician may design a new model or process that provides an incremental improvement for teaching in a specialty. There are 179 medical schools in the United States, 66 dental schools, 23 optometry schools, and 30 veterinary schools, which means that innovations for training future specialists in these fields have small markets. Interest by tech transfer offices in commercializing clinical training innovations is tepid at best.[a]

[a] One interesting exception is the growth of medical simulation; this was a revolutionary approach in clinical training. Use of simulations to support continuing education for practicing health care professionals has grown to become a $3B market in the United States.

Without a sizable existing or potential market, institutions simply cannot invest significant resources in patenting, licensing, or otherwise pushing out an invention.[16] And even if the technology passes through a number of assessment steps (see Chapter 6), finding a partner interested in licensing that technology may be problematic for niche markets. Gauging the market is something academics typically cannot do well, but it is essential to successful commercialization. Simply put, an invention that addresses an unmet need judged to be small, no matter how critical that need, may not be commercially viable. Solutions for a validated need in a market of reasonable size is *the* most important determinant of likely success and is a primary criterion by which tech transfer offices make decisions about which inventions to advance for the institution (see Box 3.2).

Culture Shift: Become an Active Partner in the Process

We have repeatedly encountered academic inventors who believe their sole responsibility is to alert the commercialization office about their inventions, and then somehow magic happens and the money starts to flow. Even worse, some believe the commercialization staff should know about their work just by reading scholarly articles or

---

Box 3.2 Drug development for rare diseases

Recognizing this disconnect, the U.S. Congress passed the Orphan Drug Act in 1983. This law provides special incentives for pharmaceutical companies to develop drugs for rare diseases, including tax breaks, expanded patent protection, and subsidies for clinical studies. It has achieved its primary aim, spurring development of new drug therapies for rare diseases; in a few cases those drugs turned out to have additional applications, and became blockbusters.[a]

[a] Sharma et al. (2010).

by trolling university websites. Not even the best-performing offices work in that way; rather, they seek to develop active partnerships with inventors.

A commitment to engage in an active partnership with the commercialization office is not trivial,[17] and the academic inventor shares equal responsibility for cultivating the relationship. The inventor knows more about the technology than anyone else, while tech transfer staff typically know more about options to move the technology down a path toward commercialization; collectively you can make connections with potential licensees. Clear, consistent, and ongoing communication between the partners is necessary for successful translation of research to the marketplace.

What does it mean to commit to engage? In Chapter 6 we list a number of best practices for the engaged academic inventor. Such individuals understand their responsibilities and have a mindset of trust in and respect for the work done by commercialization staff.

Culture Shift: New Vocabulary

Jargon is everywhere, and academics are enamored of their own. Tech transfer is no exception: it uses words and phrases that include a mix of legal and business terms as well as their own.[18] Chapter 2 introduced you to some of those phrases, such as license and term sheet. Additional expressions like bar date and value proposition, not to mention new acronyms like PCT and WIPO, are part of the commercialization landscape. We introduce the most important of these throughout the book and provide a glossary for quick reference; Box 3.3 explains why you should have a working knowledge of those terms.

Culture Shift: Different Working Norms

Research laboratories are inherently hierarchical. The group leader (referred to as the PI, or Principal Investigator in academia; the PD,

Box 3.3 Jargon, jargon everywhere

In our experience, academic inventors tend not to query tech transfer staff who use jargon. The reluctance of researchers to display their unfamiliarity with keywords, phrases, and processes leads to more misunderstandings down the line. Furthermore, some words used by researchers have very different meanings in tech transfer, leading to even more confusion, and we point out examples as they arise.

or Project Director, in other environments) sets the direction of the research, writes grant proposals, and oversees publications and conference presentations. Often there are postdoctoral scholars who have some degree of autonomy (which varies considerably among disciplines and sources of funding) and who work with students. Graduate students training for MS and PhD degrees have less autonomy still; undergraduate students, technicians, visiting scholars, high school interns, and others round out the rosters. Some lab groups are quite small, with a few students and one or two postdocs, while others can have upwards of 30 or 40 individuals. The PI is responsible for it all, and thus a hierarchical structure is needed to ensure that the work is done. Similar hierarchies occur in research groups headed by a PD in federal labs, institutes, and other quasi-academic organizations.

This hierarchical structure can impede first steps in engaging commercialization processes. In particular, a key innovation may arise from the work of a research student,[19] who is eager to explore translation and market options. That student shares credit for the invention with the PI, who may be much less eager to engage with tech transfer. The PI can either quash or encourage interest, and many a graduate student becomes disenchanted with an academic career when the PI does not commit to considering commercialization options for their work.[20] We strongly encourage faculty to provide such opportunities for their students, which can provide pathways for nonacademic careers[21] as well as amplify the societal impact of the research.

A crucial element of the commercialization environment is timeframe. You may have only a day or two to respond to a request for additional information from the commercialization office or a potential licensee. Forms must be signed and filed according to a strict schedule for IP protection. Academic research operates on a timetable that is glacial compared to business, and lack of attention to timely responses can kill license deals or complicate patent applications.[22] First-time inventors often make these elementary mistakes, whereas serial inventors come to understand the need for rapid responses.

(Possible) Personal Shift: Self-Knowledge and Humility

It's time for some tough love. Success in research requires self-confidence and tenacity because the process of peer review is unrelentingly critical, and cracking a problem in the lab can take months or years of effort.[23] Adapting to the hypercritical nature of research, academics can slide from self-confidence into hubris.[24] This plays out in several ways, including a supposed hierarchy of science, with pure math at the top and the social sciences languishing at the bottom.[25] Hubris, especially among research scientists, leads them to undervalue the skills and knowledge of those who are business- or legally-oriented. Inventors who believe they have nothing new to learn about commercialization other than technical details and vocabulary inevitably fail. Academic hubris that assumes you can transfer your knowledge and skills to the domain of tech transfer, discounting the advice of professionals in that office, is fatal.

The market is not impressed with intelligence, hard work, academic honors, or publication lists. Rather, successful commercialization requires academics to be coachable and possibly to partner with individuals who have honed skills in patent law, product development, regulatory affairs, and so on. The academic researcher must learn to trust others on the team to execute in areas for which they are themselves completely naïve or unsuited. Furthermore, such partnerships are structured differently than in research, where collaboration is built upon complementary techniques. Commercialization teams require complementary knowledge bases and skills, including interpersonal skills.

Perhaps the most difficult transition for academics to understand is that for many paths and processes they may have only supportive roles to play.[26] For many, that is just fine because they want to get back to the lab. For other inventors, however, this loss of control is a bitter pill. For example, the inventor may want more detail in the claims of a patent application than the patent attorney finds advisable. Alternatively, an inventor may have a lead to a licensee that is not acceptable to the university. An inventor's willful ignorance (= uncoachability), particularly concerning public disclosure, can impede and sometimes kill tech transfer efforts.[27] Acceptance of a supportive role requires humility and self-knowledge.

Culture Shift: Different Value Systems

Let's start with commonalities. Academic and commercialization cultures share an emphasis on high-quality scholarship: second-rate research is unlikely to lead to an innovation that finds a market.[28] Thus, academic researchers must be convinced of the intrinsic value of their work in order to pitch it to outside interests, whether through a discussion with a potential licensee, a company interested in sponsoring research, or potential customers of a start-up company. The inventor's personal passion for the research that led to an innovative breakthrough is a primary value that translates well from academia to marketplace.

The cultures diverge, though, in numerous ways. First, we iterate the concept of time: markets move at rapid clips. Industry sponsors may insist on meeting benchmarks within shorter timeframes than academics are used to, and investors may want proof-of-concept progress within a few short months. In such cases, academics must adjust to a highly accelerated timeframe.

Second, the world of commercialization requires that academics learn to communicate in fundamentally different ways. In Chapter 6, we describe the kinds of communications that are needed to start various processes, and we urge you to use straightforward language in written documents. Usually, it is easier for the legal team to learn science and engineering than it is for you to learn law,[29] which in itself may be a bitter pill!

Third, the academic reward system does not translate well to commercialization activity (Chapter 1). Scholarly publications, conferences, and funding are the coins of the academic realm. In most academic units, participating in commercialization steps is viewed as "extra credit" rather than fundamental metrics of career success. Because faculty keenly tune into the rewards structure,[30] some institutions have started to amend personnel policies to include invention disclosures, patents filed, and the like.[31] Standards for promotion and tenure remain rooted in academic values and metrics, and commercialization is only slowly creeping in.[32] We offer suggestions for administrators on how to more closely align the two systems in the Epilogue.

Conclusion

Moving your discovery out of the institution requires that you work with new teams, especially people in the tech transfer office. Some shifts in your thinking and behavior, which are actually rather minor, can make you a more effective partner. Expanding your mindset to apply concepts from the worlds of business and law to your technology facilitates communication with commercialization colleagues, and allows you to adjust to a new environment. By becoming a willing and informed partner, you really can change the world!

PROFILE: Katalin Karikó

Katalin Karikó is a molecular biologist who became intrigued with the idea of using messenger RNA (mRNA) for therapeutic purposes more than 30 years ago. Messenger RNA is produced within cells by encoding information in DNA, and it directs the production of proteins. Her work paved the way for use of synthetic mRNA to prime the immune system of a host (like you and us) against viruses. mRNA vaccines are in widespread use for the first time as we battle the SARS-CoV-2 virus that causes COVID-19.

In the 1990s, Karikó was a professor at the University of Pennsylvania (Penn), embedded within a culture that prized NIH funding and publications. She wrote numerous grant proposals; but did not receive substantial funding because she had not found a way to prevent the immune system from attacking the mRNA itself. In 1995 she was denied promotion and worse, was demoted. Yet she persisted.[1]

Karikó enlisted immunologist Drew Weissman as a collaborator, along with others. Together, the team discovered that by tweaking the mRNA molecules, they could get synthetic mRNA into cells without provoking an immune response. This fundamental discovery, published in 2005 (and not widely recognized then), set the stage for additional work in numerous market focus areas. The first promising application was use of synthetic mRNA to re-program somatic cells to become stem cells, which attracted the attention of other scientists and venture capitalists. Indeed, prior to the pandemic, there were more than 500 mRNA clinical trials underway for more than 20 disease categories— none of them infectious disease vaccines[2]. Among those who saw promise in the technology were

Beyond Discovery. Jean E. Schelhorn and Joan M. Herbers, Oxford University Press. © Oxford University Press 2022. DOI: 10.1093/oso/9780197512715.003.0006

the founders of two companies called BioNTech and Moderna—companies that today are making big headlines.

More of the backstory: Karikó and Weissman were inventors on an issued patent assigned to trustees of the University of Pennsylvania and founded a company, RNARx. That start-up was awarded a STTR Fast-Track grant (Phase I and II) but folded after a few years; Penn then licensed the technology to a Wisconsin biotech firm. A different team saw possibilities for the new mRNA technology in cancer immunotherapy. They founded the company BioNTech, and within a few years recruited Karikó to join the company as senior vice president (after Penn refused to give her a faculty appointment). She now is a named inventor on patent applications assigned to BioNTech. Karikó and her collaborator Weissman were awarded the 2021 Albany and Lasker Prizes for their groundbreaking work.

When the pandemic happened, mRNA technology was sufficiently advanced to be deployed. Early in 2020, both Moderna and BioNTech pivoted to mRNA vaccine development to fight COVID-19, the disease caused by SARS-CoV-2. Moderna produced its own vaccine, while BioNTech formed a partnership with Pfizer to develop and distribute a second one. Both companies created vaccines with high efficacy at lightning speed and have received emergency use authorization in multiple countries, including the United States.[3]

4

Behind the Curtain: A Glimpse into the World of Intellectual Property

Much of the academic's creative output is intentionally *not* protected, in line with the value of free and open sharing of ideas. In this chapter we introduce you to the topic of intellectual property. In the following chapters, we build on these basics to present situations in which you as an academic are required to initiate action: *it is vital for researchers to understand their responsibilities to report inventions.* Furthermore, we describe ways you can support institutional processes set up to protect intellectual property. If you wish to actively contribute to translating your findings to the marketplace and/ or think you might become an entrepreneur, this chapter is for you.

Academic researchers often use the term *intellectual property* to describe their ideas, research protocols, teaching materials, and research results. However, many of those intellectual assets are not in fact IP. Intellectual property (IP) has a tight legal definition, and in this chapter we make explicit what falls into that category (What is IP?). We also describe the basis for interest in IP protection in the commercial world (Why does it matter?), as well as paths available to protect IP (How is it done?).[1] Pursuing IP protection is a practice that involves numerous parties, both inside and outside your institution. You as the inventor have specific responsibilities (detailed in the next two chapters), while your tech transfer office takes the lead. The tech transfer office (for which we use the shorthand TTO, understanding full well that at your institution it might be called something different or may even be housed outside) may choose to bring

Beyond Discovery. Jean E. Schelhorn and Joan M. Herbers, Oxford University Press. © Oxford University Press 2022. DOI: 10.1093/oso/9780197512715.003.0007

in external parties, such as patent lawyers. If you have the pleasure of actually working with teams seeking to protect your inventions/discoveries/insights through formal IP development activities, you will learn over time and grow in your proficiency.[2] The complexity of intellectual property is daunting, so let's get started on the fundamentals you should master.

What Is Intellectual Property?

Intellectual property includes filed patent applications, issued patents (maintained in force), trademarks, trade dress, copyrighted items, and in some cases trade secrets. In most countries, these categories are options for legal protection, for nonobvious insights, inventions, ornamental features of products, works of authorship, artwork, and new plant varieties.

Academics are well versed in copyright protection for authors/creators, including permissible use and the need to seek permissions. Gaining copyright protection is easy and within the control of the creator. U.S. law recognizes the existence of copyright in a work at the moment of its creation in a tangible medium of expression. Note that it is no longer required to make the simple well-known declaration including "copyright" (or the copyright symbol ©), the date, and the owner's name for copyright to exist as a legal right. However, the rights in copyright are practically enforceable only when it is the subject of a formal filing in the U.S. Copyright Office, which is the copyright owner's ticket to the federal courthouse if enforcement is needed. Given that this is not likely to be new ground for you, we do not treat copyright-protected IP in depth (but see Box 4.1 for a recent complication).[3] Similarly, we do not cover trademarks,[4] trade dress,[5] or trade secrets[6] in depth but focus primarily on patentable IP.

Patent and copyright legalities differ in several crucial respects. While both require the applicant to make a filing with the federal government to secure enforceable rights, one can obtain copyright registration in a matter of months by simply filing with the

---

Box 4.1 Online instruction prompted by COVID-19

Copyright complications have arisen with the advent of online-every-thing in higher education during the COVID-19 pandemic. Teaching staff have had to move their courses from in-person to remote instruction, and many faculty videotaped class sessions for students to use as needed. Yet online programs have been available for more than 20 years. Because distance-learning courses are prepared with the support of dedicated staff as well as instructors, the institution itself has a claim on copyrighted materials used online. Taped lectures and other materials prepared in the COVID-19 environment are similar, and the convention in higher education that copyright on teaching materials is held by the instructor may not transfer to online teaching. That fear prompted the American Association of University Professors (AAUP) to release a position statement specifically exempting them from such claims.[a] Particularly useful is a distinction between distance learning (institutionally branded distance education programs) and remote learning (instructor-led posting of class materials during COVID-19).

[a] https://www.aaup.org/news/aft-and-aaup-principles-higher-education-response-covid-19#.YA74wS1h2NG.

---

government and satisfying the formalities of the application at a modest cost. Filing a patent application, however, provides no assurance of eventual patent protection and requires a more extensive (and expensive) examination process that can take years. Although both copyright and patent holders may need to sue in federal court to stop infringers, copyright registration when done promptly enables copyright owners to claim statutory damages and attorney's fees from infringers. By contrast, patent owners must always prove damages and can recover attorney's fees only in exceptional cases.

IP rights in the United States are based on language in the U.S. Constitution.[7] This resulted in a body of statutes enacted by Congress to create the patent, trademark and copyright systems that secure those rights to authors and inventors.

In the United States, as in most of the world, the first inventor to file for a patent on an invention is entitled to a patent if the invention, after thorough assessment, is found at the time of the invention to be new, useful, and nonobvious to one skilled in the art. When a patent is allowed and issued, it secures to the inventor a set of legal rights, including the right to exclude others from making, using, selling, offering to sell, or importing the invention.[8] The inventor is highlighted here: numerous inventors can be named on a patent, and in most cases academic researchers are under an obligation to assign the rights in their inventions and other research results to the academic institution that employs them.[9] The academic institution, as the assignee, then has the legal rights to pursue a patent. The assignee institution may, in turn, have an obligation to assign or license rights to the federal government, another funding entity, or collaborator pursuant to grants, funding, and/or research agreements.[10]

In exchange for the rights granted, U.S. patent laws require inventors to fully disclose the invention, teach the details of how the invention is practiced, and set forth a best mode of practicing the invention in the patent. This "requirement to teach" allows the invention to be fully practiced by others once the patent expires, is abandoned, or is no longer in force,[11] at which time the invention and information contained in the patent enter the public domain.

All patents involve legal processes to file an application and work toward issuance. This process is referred to as patent prosecution and includes multiple steps: filing, engaging with a patent examiner who works for a government, and paying fees as the application advances. The entire process to obtain a patent can take from one to six years to complete, depending on how aggressively the owner of the invention proceeds,[12] and it typically requires engagement of specialized patent lawyers or patent agents.[13] Involving professionals who know the terrain of patent prosecution is essential. The creator/inventor plays important roles in many steps, while others, especially those in the TTO, have critical development and decision-making responsibilities. In Chapter 6 we highlight best practices the inventor should consider to improve chances of success in moving through decision steps and to develop solid working relationships with TTO professionals.

In this chapter more so than in any other part of this book, we describe very specific rules, requirements, and terminology. Please be aware that we are just skimming the surface and focusing on patents! The process of patent protection is a complex, ever-evolving area of the law and can involve a significant number of strategic, legal, and commercial decisions. You will find that getting the details right is as important in a patent application as it is in an experiment. Your technology transfer team (which may include in-house or external patent attorneys) has in-depth expertise that likely is necessary to protect key aspects of your concepts and inventions. Our goal is to provide you with enough perspective so that you understand why and when to seek help, as well as when and how you must contribute to specific steps.

Why Are Patents of Interest?

Patent applications and issued patents are not commercialization per se, nor are they always needed for successful commercialization. An issued U.S. patent grants the inventor(s) or their assignee(s) the right to exclude others[14] for a legally defined period from making, using, selling, or offering to sell, or importing[15] the process, machine, article of manufacture, or composition of matter, or any new and useful improvement thereof that are covered in one or more of the issued claims of a patent in force in the United States. Other countries grant similar rights to exclude. This is the "what" for patents: an issued patent allows the patent owner to exclude others from making, using, selling, or importing the specific inventive elements described in the patent claims. There is a time limit for this right to exclude— more on that below.

The "why" for patents is that they provide a competitive edge in potential marketplaces. Exclusivity can be a powerful business advantage. If the development cycle for a given product or manufacturing platform requires significant capital and time, the assurance of a time period for excluding others from use of a patented invention is often an absolute requirement for the business decision to invest in that development. The value of a patent is twofold: it protects time and investment in product development, testing, approval, and market launch; and it protects time thereafter for exclusive sales in the market.[16]

The actual time period of exclusion (enforcement period) depends on the type of patent. Patents are issued in three categories: (1) a *utility patent* protects the claimed process, machine, article of manufacture, or composition of matter, or any new and useful improvement thereof;[17] (2) a *design patent* protects ornamental characteristics of a manufactured article or ornamental features on an article;[18] and (3) a *plant paten*t protects a new asexually reproducing plant variety.[19] Of these three categories, the most important for academic commercialization by far is the utility patent.[20]

For plant patents and utility patents, the patent life is 20 years from the date of first filing; the period the patent is actually in force and enforceable is 20 years minus the years/months/days between patent application filing date and the patent issue date, plus any period of delay in patent prosecution due to the U.S. Patent and Trademark Office (USPTO); an illustrative example is given in Box 4.2. As we describe later in the chapter, filing a patent application establishes a priority date, but no enforcement is possible until a patent issues.

Box 4.2 Patent life realities

Your institution files a utility patent application, which takes three years to prosecute prior to issuance. A licensee has a grant of rights to this patent as a critical component of a new product. The licensee takes six years from patent issuance to develop the product, secure regulatory approval, create manufacturing capability, and launch the product. Sales start slowly and accelerate in year 3 following product launch. At this point, 12 years of patent life have been consumed and 8 remain for the licensee to manufacture and sell the patented product, recoup development costs, pay royalties to the licensor, and make a profit. When the patent expires, competitors can enter the market with comparable products.

Once the patent life is over, royalty revenue for the patent to the licensor ends, unless it is accrued from sales of materials that were in the licensee inventory (and thus "made") prior to patent expiration. Thereafter, the licensee can continue manufacturing and selling the product with no further obligation to pay the licensor under the license to the patent and no rights to exclude potential competitors; the patent is now in the public domain. Thus, for example, a pharmaceutical company can enter the market with a generic drug after the patent covering the previously patented composition of matter expires.[21]

What Types of Inventions Can Be Patented?

As mentioned previously, patent protection is offered in these legally defined categories:

Utility Patents[22]

- process
- machine
- manufacture
- composition of matter
- any new and useful improvement thereof

Design Patents[23]

- new, original, and ornamental design for an article of manufacture

Plant Patents[24]

- plant varieties that reproduce asexually, including cultivated sports, mutants, hybrids, and newly found seedlings, other than a tuber

For the rest of this chapter, we focus on utility patents.

What Is the Structure of a Patent Application?

A patent has three parts: abstract, specification, and claims. The claims are crucial: they set forth elements that define the subject matter of an issued patent. Claims are what is actually protected, and they define the exclusionary rights afforded to the owner when they are enforced.[25] Claims are typically written by patent lawyers and must be based on information in the specification. The specification is broadly written to include all material necessary to fully describe the invention and enable its use, whereas the claims describe what is protected and are narrower than the specification. The patent specification generally includes references, background information, definitions used, the unmet need being addressed, experimental details and results, and the uses for the technology/inventions. Again, the patent system provides for a grant of exclusive rights in exchange for disclosure, so all patents must include enough specifics to teach a "person skilled in the art" how to practice the invention.

The Path to an Issued Patent: Patent Prosecution

The specific goal of the patent applicant is to obtain allowance of claims that are broad enough in scope to be of commercial value.[26] Filing a patent application initiates a series of steps leading to an exchange between the patent applicant (the inventor(s) or assignee) and a government patent examiner to move the application along a path toward "allowed claims."[27] Written communications from the examiner, referred to as office actions, require a response from the applicant. The communications focus on three statutory criteria that must be met in order for the claimed subject matter to be allowable. The subject matter must be:

- new,
- useful, and

- nonobvious to one skilled in the art at the time of filing the invention.

Patent examiners and patent attorneys often use the terms *novelty*, *utility*, and *nonobviousness* to describe these requirements.

Determining if the claims meet these criteria may sound simple. However, the patentability criteria are applied with reference to all "prior art" that existed before the priority date. Prior art refers to the publicly available body of work that is documented in some form anywhere in the world. So, prior art includes information in published patent applications, patents, journal articles, abstracts, posters, recorded presentations, books, text/image information available on the internet, and other articles, *including your own*. Prior art is therefore an extremely broad category. You are likely knowledgeable about relevant prior art residing in scholarly outlets but may not be aware of prior art in other forms. We will refer to the prior art topic in the prosecution steps below and more broadly in Chapter 6.

Once a decision to pursue patent protection is made, input from you will be pivotal in the patent filing (Chapter 6). The legal team seeks to file the strongest patent application[28] possible by crafting claims for the patent filing that set forth elements defining the invention in a way that avoids claiming prior art.

Searches to identify the prior art relevant to an invention are not required of the patent applicant as part of the filing. However, the patent applicant has a duty to report prior art that the inventor and applicant are aware of and that is relevant to the invention.[29] A list of such known prior art is typically submitted shortly after the patent application is filed. During patent prosecution, the inventor and applicant are also required to supplement any prior art information they find. The inventor should be periodically reminded of this obligation by the TTO or the assigned lawyer.

A TTO can file a patent application without in-depth prior art searches.[30] In other situations, a search for relevant art information can be obtained (by the inventor or TTO staff) and provided to the patent lawyer for consideration in drafting the patent application specification and claims. And in some instances official law firm searches are commissioned, and confidential patentability opinions[31] are rendered before decisions are made to draft and file the case. The bottom line is: while the requirement is that you disclose prior art of which you are aware, proactive searches can be very helpful both for making the decision to file for a patent and for drafting the application. The patent examiners will do searches as the case is examined, and a proactive search may allow you to anticipate the art that must be navigated during subsequent prosecution steps. In sum, searches of prior art support several goals: they inform the decision to file; they provide information for drafting the application; and they allow you to envision how prosecution may proceed.

Once filed (and now in prosecution), the patent application moves into detailed examination by the patent office for the country in which the application was filed. The patent office conducts a thorough review, searches the prior art (including prior art references cited in the application), and issues a search report.[32] The search report provides prior art references associated with claims in the application and categorized as relevant to novelty (inventive step), or nonobviousness (sometimes in combination with additional references); other references may cite technological background. If the filing is made in the USPTO, the first office action is accompanied by a search, and the examiner states reasons why the claims are or are not allowable. This and subsequent office actions require responses and are time-sensitive. Search report results provide a heads-up concerning issues that must be resolved before a patent can issue. As the first communication in prosecution, the search report allows the applicant to prepare for subsequent office actions.

Office actions center on examination of the claims. The original claim set as filed in an application is typically amended as the case moves through prosecution. Note that claims can be amended in prosecution but the specification cannot.[33] Patent attorneys therefore spend substantial effort to ensure that the specification fully discloses the invention so that it will hold up throughout prosecution. Office actions from the examiner describe the official view of the government patent office of why your patent claims do or do not meet the criteria for patentability (novelty, nonobviousness, utility), based on its search and interpretation of the relevant prior art. In responding to the office action, the applicant team makes the argument as to why the prior art references cited do not negate the patentability of each claim. Claim amendment may also be needed[34] as a result of the art cited, arguments raised by the examiner, and legal aspects of claim construction. Patent prosecution typically proceeds through an exchange of formal written documents, but it is possible for the patent counsel to schedule an in-person meeting or a conversation on the phone; the participation of an inventor may be requested as well. Such person-to-person discussions are especially helpful to demonstrate or illustrate the nonobvious features of inventions. After numerous communications, the patent examiner may agree to allow specific wording of amended claims, and if the applicant is in agreement, at this point the patent application is "allowed." Finally, upon payment of an issue fee, the patent is issued and published.[35]

Case law concerning patentable matter changes over time (Box 4.3). Lawyers stay current and can provide the level of knowledge and strategic input to position claims in light of what is acceptable. As a result, patent strategies employed in the past to allow claims may no longer be viable paths; patents allowed previously and still in force may not, under current patent law, be enforceable. Conversely, new case law can give new life to patents whose value was believed to be destroyed by other decisions.[36]

Filing Strategy

In an ideal situation, a patent application is prepared in a measured fashion. A patent lawyer or patent agent is engaged, and all pertinent materials are carefully considered (searching, identifying, and assessing prior art). A patent filing decision is based on business, legal, and technical input, and a filing strategy is considered. A patent application is carefully drafted and reviewed multiple times with inventor input, and the filing strategy is refined. This takes time.

Box 4.3 Patent law is not static

Case law states that "anything under the sun that is made by man"[a] can be patented. Thus, naturally occurring materials and laws of nature cannot be patented.[b] Additionally, the courts have also held that abstract ideas cannot be patented.[c] The subject matter of patentability is constantly being challenged at the edges as new technologies arise and new tools are developed. Software, inventions developed using artificial intelligence, and the ability to synthesize DNA have led to inventions that do not fit neatly into traditional categories.[d] These examples illustrate how case law has changed over the years, causing the matter eligible for patent protection to evolve over time.

[a] *Diamond v. Chakrabarty* (1980).
[b] *Mayo Collaborative Services v. Prometheus Laboratories Inc.* (2012).
[c] *Bilski v Kappos* (2010).
[d] A recent interesting example, *Roche v. Cepheid* (2018), established that DNA primers cannot be patented. These constructs include naturally occurring DNA, with tag ends added to promote replication. The Court determined that adding those tags did not sufficiently change the product from its natural state.

However, some situations require that an application be filed quickly, which can be accomplished with a provisional patent application filing strategy. A provisional is a quick route for filing and does not require a full set of patent claims. It establishes a priority date for the information filed, and the filed information then can subsequently be developed into a utility patent application. Even so, it is best to completely disclose the invention through a fully developed provisional patent application, as this step establishes a priority date for the matter contained in it. A key rule to understand is that provisional patent applications expire one year from their filing date and are not published. To be of any value, they must be converted to a formal utility patent filing within that one-year period. Throughout that year, additional information can be incorporated into a new provisional application if deemed necessary, and that information receives its own priority date.

Box 4.4 Urgent timelines limit options

An inventor prepares a poster for a meeting and shares it with the TTO a few days before it is scheduled for presentation. The TTO may decide to file a provisional patent application based on the poster, which establishes a priority date for this matter. The poster itself will likely be the key content in the filing, and the inventor may be asked to provide any associated materials that are available, and those materials will likely be included. Although not required, including claims in the provisional will help associate claims with the priority date. If additional data are obtained and presented to the TTO three months later, the TTO may now elect to aggregate the new and previously filed information into a utility patent application. The two sets of information have different priority dates despite being in the same subsequent utility filing.

The example in Box 4.4 illustrates a key reason for the provisional filing strategy: to avoid the negative consequences of an enabling public disclosure. We treat public disclosure in depth in Chapter 6. For now, we point out that very few countries in the world (the United States being one of them) allow a patent application to be filed within 12 months after a public disclosure. *In most countries, a public disclosure negates the ability to file a patent application* because the invention has already been given to the public domain. Since you control with whom, where, and how you talk about your research to others, the issue of public disclosure merits full consideration![37]

A provisional patent filing can serve several other functions. For example, if a priority date is critical *and* additional enabling results are expected soon, one can possibly be the first to file on a concept[38] (priority date established) while the researcher is still collecting data to support that concept. In this case, the inventor has roughly 8 months to produce those data, giving the TTO/patent professionals time to incorporate them into the specification of a full utility application before the 12-month filing deadline. Alternatively, if the required data do not support the case, the filing can be abandoned. In such a case, the original filing is unpublished and does not constitute prior art for any subsequent filing.

Another example involves cases for which multiple priority dates may be advantageously obtained for multiple inventions in a rapidly evolving area of research. In this case, multiple provisional applications may be aggregated into one utility patent application within the one-year time period from the first filed provisional application. Finally, it may be advantageous for even a fully developed patent application to be filed as a provisional application, simply to allow an opportunity to add further information or adjust claims prior to becoming a formal utility application. In sum, provisional patent applications have multiple uses and are frequently filed by companies and research entities alike, including academic institutions and federal labs.

In contrast to a provisional patent filing, the institution can submit a comprehensive utility patent application as the first filing. As we emphasized earlier, utility patent applications must be fully developed and carefully prepared. In the specification, the details of the experiments and experimental results leading to the invention and the invention itself are fully articulated, and care is taken to ensure that the most current information is reflected.

The final strategic issue we discuss is the international patent filing decision: *where* to file (in just the United States, or both the United States and internationally, or just outside the United States). Global interest in simplifying and unifying international filing steps led to the Patent Cooperation Treaty (PCT), signed in 1970 and administered by the World Intellectual Property Organization (WIPO), which provides a means for one patent application filed in the PCT to be recognized as a valid patent filing in all countries that are parties to the treaty. For many institutions, a PCT filing is the first step toward possible filings in multiple participant countries. Currently, 153 countries are participating in the Patent Cooperatiion Treaty,[39] including the United States. One can file directly into the PCT, or the PCT filing can be made simultaneously with or after a direct national filing into any of the PCT countries, as long as the PCT filing is made within 12 months from the initial filing.

Filing into the PCT allows the applicant to file the patent application later as a national patent application in any of the PCT countries.[40] The PCT process provides that such individual national filings can be made at any time prior to the 30–34 month deadline from the date of first filing, depending on the country.[41] This is referred to as the PCT "national stage election" deadline, and filing into any of these countries is the second international filing decision that must be made. Each country into which a national filing is made retains the authority under its own laws to search the prior art, prosecute the patent application, potentially issue the patent, and collect relevant fees. Each country also has specific filing criteria (translations, legal construction, etc.), necessitating a knowledgeable patent lawyer in each country. One other unique aspect of filing in the PCT is its issue of a publicly available search report at 18 months from the first filing (with no response from the applicant required, in contrast to a USPTO-issued search report).

Filing with the PCT is the most efficient means to buy time while the TTO considers whether or not to make additional national filings. If, on the other hand. the applicant knows exactly which countries are of interest, there may be no need to undertake the PCT process. Note that alternatively, an applicant can file individual national patent applications outside the United States within 12 months of the first filing date of the U.S. patent application (provisional or regular filing).

For TTOs, the decision on where to file is strongly influenced by the presence or absence of a license agreement. Some TTO offices only file with the PCT if a license agreement is in place that includes terms for paying patent costs and directing the country selection. Some TTO offices may move to a PCT filing if there is evidence of large international markets or manufacturing capability in countries for which patent filings are sought, even if a licensee is not yet identified. However, the most common scenario is that, without a licensee in place, the TTO is likely to make limited filings.

What Patent Protection Does not Do

Patent prosecution establishes if claims can be allowed, and you now know that claims are allowed that reflect the inventive subject matter in the patent application that is deemed to be new, nonobvious, and useful. What the process does not tell you is whether the claims lie within claims of other patents (whether in force or not). That is, the prosecution process does not inform the assignee and its licensees if they have the ability to *practice* the claims. This consideration leads us to discussion of patent infringement and patent enforcement.

The ability to *practice* the claims is not guaranteed by virtue of issuing a patent.[42] This can become critical for a licensee moving to product development: it is a significant business consideration. The central question is whether the patent rights infringe other patents, and this topic forms the basis for many interesting stories in the news. The electronics industry with its many semiconductor patents and improvements thereon is an apt example of the potential patent thicket that must be navigated as products are developed.

The issuance of a patent does not guarantee others will willingly refrain from practicing the claimed invention. Patent infringement can occur in several ways, but in its simplest form, it occurs when an unlicensed party practices the claims of an issued, in-force patent.[43] If the patent is not yet licensed, the act of informing the second party that a patent exists and is in force (a first step in enforcement[44]) could encourage that party/entity to license the patent. If the patent is already licensed by a TTO, typically the license agreement requires the licensee to enforce the patent rights as a condition of the license agreement. Regardless, after providing notice to an alleged infringer, a second step in enforcement (if negotiation to stop, license, or sublicense a patent is unsuccessful) may be litigation in federal court (example in Box 4.5).

The TTO and its licensee(s) can have a keen interest in patent enforcement actions, as the example above illustrates. If a case for possible infringement is strong, the party responsible for patent enforcement—the TTO or its licensee, or both—can ask those parties to stop practicing the invention before filing suit. If the patent is not

---

Box 4.5 Infringement litigation for a plant patent

An interesting infringement case concerns a plant patent. The University of California—Davis (UCD) has an active program developing new plant cultivars for various crops important to the state, and many of those cultivars are patented. California Berry Cultivars (CBC) lost an infringement suit in 2017 brought by UCD for selling strawberries derived from UCD's patented cultivars without a license. Driscoll, a large strawberry-growing firm, watched that infringement suit and realized that CBC also was selling fruit that may have infringed Driscoll's patents; Driscoll filed suit in March 2019 and the case is pending.

---

yet licensed, the TTO can seek a license from the other party for future use and additional compensation for past use of the issued patent. If the patent is already licensed, the license agreement may allow the licensee to issue a sublicense. Without such enforcement, others can practice claims with impunity. Not surprisingly, many companies and increasingly many academic centers are vigilant to enforce their patents.[45]

Finally, we come to the topic of patent invalidity. Patents and individual patent claims can be invalidated for numerous reasons, and patents may be invalidated through proceedings in the USPTO or in the federal courts. One reason for invalidation is the discovery of prior art that (1) by definition, existed prior to the patent's priority date, (2) was not considered in prosecution, and (3) would likely have influenced claim allowance if it had been considered; a timely example is given in Box 4.6.

Additional means of patent invalidation include proof of use, offer for sale, actual sale, or an enabling public disclosure more than 12 months before valid filing of a patent application in the United States.[46]

A final reason for invalidation can be improperly naming inventors on a patent: attention to details about inventorship is crucial.[47] It is important to understand that inventorship is not

---

Box 4.6 Patent invalidation is a serious topic

In July 2020 Moderna, seeking to bring a SARS-CoV-2 vaccine to the market, lost a bid to invalidate a U.S. patent owned by Arbutus Biopharma on the basis of obviousness. Moderna had received rights to the patent of interest through a licensee of Arbutus but clearly saw aspects of the situation as problematic and sought to invalidate the patent. Thus far, the patent has not been invalidated, and Arbutus could receive royalties derived from a Moderna vaccine, which is now in distribution and use.[a] The financial implications of this fight are obvious, and it is expected to go into appeal.[b] Years may pass before it is resolved. A second complication is that the Moderna vaccine (and others) was developed in part with funding from the U.S. federal government, yet Moderna did not disclose that fact on its patent applications.[c] As we explain in Chapter 5, such funding carries with it the stipulation that the government retains the rights to any IP produced from that funding. The pandemic landscape has exposed many IP-related topics, including government ownership of vaccines.[d]

[a] https://www.evaluate.com/vantage/articles/news/patents-and-litigation/covid-19-vaccine-battle-just-got-interesting; https://www.biospace.com/article/moderna-loses-patent-challenge-with-arbutus-on-vaccine-technology https://www.forbes.com/sites/nathanvardi/2020/07/29/modernas-mysterious-coronavirus-vaccine-delivery-system/#6079959562d9.

[b] One of the authors is reminded of the wise words of her father: "Jean, you will only know the value of your patents when they are tested in court." So true!

[c] https://www.statnews.com/pharmalot/2020/08/28/moderna-covid19-vaccine-coronavirus-patents-darpa

[d] https://news.bloomberglaw.com/pharma-and-life-sciences/government-may-have-ownership-or-rights-to-coronavirus-vaccines

---

equivalent to authorship. Academic researchers are often generous with co-authorship on publications, but inventorship cannot actually be determined by anyone (such as the principal investigator) engaged with the invention. Determining inventorship involves a legal and factual analysis made by a patent attorney.

An inventor is one who materially contributes to the inventive concept as ultimately reduced to practice and claimed in the issued patent.[48] Inventorship should be established by patent attorneys at two points: the first is at the time of patent filing, when inventor names are submitted with the filing materials; and the second—when determining inventorship becomes absolutely critical—is when claims are allowed and before the patent is issued. Following a notice of allowance and prior to payment of the fees needed to issue a patent, a patent attorney should review the allowed claims to confirm if the originally named inventors listed on the first filing should remain as filed or be amended in view of the allowed claims. Inventors should be added or deleted as necessary to reflect their contributors to the allowed claims. For example, narrowing the list of inventors often occurs where a team has been involved in research and a broad patent specification is written that encompasses multiple inventions, but only one invention is present in the allowed claims. Unfortunately, neither point of review is routinely formalized in many academic institutions, although it is common in the for-profit world. Inventors named or not named on an issued patent can be challenged through court action, and the wrong names (whether added or omitted) can invalidate the patent. Proper inventorship is a legal requirement.

A Bit about Costs

The answer to "how much do patents cost?" is, not surprisingly, "it depends." The overall costs of filing and issuing a patent in a single country is highly variable, averaging from US$15,000 to $30,000, depending on many factors. These costs themselves consist of fixed and variable components. Fixed costs are the government fees. Such fees are charged in the United States (and in every other country where a patent filing occurs) during prosecution and through the life of the patent. Variable costs include labor performed by patent attorneys or agents and their foreign legal affiliates (as required). Attorney fees themselves are highly variable, depending on the individual's experience, the technological field, complexity of the case, and location of the firm (e.g., charges for U.S. patent attorney time are considerably higher in metropolitan areas and near technology hot spots like Silicon Valley and Boston than elsewhere). Many websites provide a range of total costs for utility filings. Recall that this is a very early step in the path toward an issued patent. Every step in the process after the filing has its own fixed and variable costs.[49]

In the United States, the initial filing fee for a provisional patent application, at its simplest, could cost as little as $140 (in 2021).[50] Thereafter, costs escalate, and an estimate of the cost to prepare and file a fully drafted provisional application is $8,000 to $12,000.[51] The subsequent utility filing itself incurs the costs of legal services described above and has its own government fee. The USPTO sends the search report with the first office action. This and every subsequent office action requires additional fees to continue prosecution, and each such step requires services from the legal team as well. Furthermore, there can be multiple office actions during prosecution. Finally, at the end of prosecution, should claims be allowed, a patent issues only if a fee is paid; thereafter, there are scheduled fees to maintain the patent in force through the life of the patent.[52]

The simplest way to file internationally is via the PCT. Filing with the PCT incurs a $3500 fee (in 2021) and additional variable costs involving patent attorneys. Thereafter, electing to file national stage

---

Box 4.7 Institutional costs in patent portfolios

Additional costs that you may not have considered are the institutional costs, such as internal staff time and costs within the TTO to develop and manage the patent portfolio.[a] Staff salaries, external counsel, administrative costs of running the TTO office, salaries of others like university attorneys who may be consulted, and the like are real, albeit indirect, costs[b] of filing patent applications for the institution.

[a] The majority of TTOs use external counsel for patents, which entails numerous communications.
[b] The analogy to indirect costs on grants is obvious.

patent applications under the PCT multiply both fixed and variable costs by the number of countries where the matter is filed. Each country has a fee schedule and specific requirements. Each office action in each country where the application has been filed typically requires, roughly, an additional US$3,000–5,000 (primarily legal hours but also the government fees). In addition, a patent attorney must be retained in that country (as well as other professionals like translators) to ensure that the prosecution adheres to that country's laws.

At every such step, the TTO must evaluate whether it is in the institution's best interest to proceed. A rule of thumb is that 10% of all issued patents are commercially relevant.[53] Simply put, if there is no commercial interest in the invention/technology,[54] the TTO is unlikely to support these costs over time. Your TTO may offer early protection for an invention, but to keep the matter alive through additional prosecution, a licensee is a must. Because the licensee typically must pay historic and ongoing patent costs, their input drives many of the patent portfolio decisions. In short, if you want to move toward an issued patent, you should commit to helping your TTO secure a licensee, as we describe in Chapter 6.

Box 4.8 Realities of patent costs for an institution

Consider a small institution with 150 research-intensive faculty, a third of whom are active inventors. Suppose that in a given year all of those 50 report stellar discoveries/inventions. The costs to file utility patents for these 50 inventions could average $400,000–$600,000 just in year one. Suppose all of these matters move to the PCT and U.S. filings are deferred until the national stage election deadline in 30–34 months. Entering the PCT on these 50 cases costs on average an additional $200,000 or so (with case adjustments by attorneys on some of them). Now the sunk cost is $600,000–$800,000 for this one year of cases—just to file.[a]

---

[a] There are processes (with associated costs) to accelerate examinations that are not factored into this example.

Most institutions simply cannot bear the year-over-year annual filing costs of this magnitude. While some TTOs have budgets for annual patent costs, all of them engage in internal deliberations concerning which inventions to pursue for patent protection. The likelihood of finding a licensee is a major consideration because the licensor institution cannot only recover historic filing costs but also shifts costs of further prosecution to the licensee.

Conclusion

Clearly, the topic of IP protection is exceedingly complex. For every generalization there are complications and exceptions; for many of the challenges encountered, a talented professional can identify a workaround. We are not lawyers[55] and certainly we are not offering legal advice. Our overview has left out the contents of entire textbooks on intellectual property.[56] Rather, this glimpse into IP and patent prosecution should help you understand more about what the TTO and their attorney teams do. Furthermore, we trust it has convinced you that as an academic you should absolutely not attempt to call the shots on patent prosecution: do not second-guess professional advice you may receive, but do plan to be an active partner!

Once you alert the TTO of your invention, they are responsible for considering and acting to secure possible IP protection. We urge you to remain invested in their efforts and to keep the lines of communication open, as we cover thoroughly in Chapter 6. In particular, your participation at key points during patent prosecution can be decisive to the outcome. We hope you are awarded that first issued patent and go on to secure many more; more importantly, we hope you and your institution are successful attracting a licensee to commercialize the technologies!

PROFILE: Ashim Mitra

Ashim Mitra was a senior faculty member in the School of Pharmacy at the University of Missouri—Kansas City (UMKC). An expert on treatment of eye diseases, Mitra was a star, attracting substantial funding from the National Institutes of Health, state and nonprofit grants, and industrial funding. He had extensive experience with commercialization, and by 2017 had been a named inventor on 11 issued patents. He also served on the University's patent committee, which made recommendations about technologies the institution should prioritize for commercialization.

Mitra ran a large lab, which included about 20 graduate students, one of whom was Kishore Cholkar. As a doctoral student, Cholkar was assigned to investigate the problem of nanoparticle delivery of drugs. He worked for several years perfecting the technology and earned a PhD in 2015 for his dissertation, "Topical Clear Aqueous Nanomicellar Formulations For Anterior and Posterior Ocular Drug Delivery." To complete his research, Cholkar was supported, at least in part, by federal grants, and he used UMKC facilities.

Cholkar's foundational work ultimately led to the drug Cequa[TM], which was approved by the U.S. Food and Drug Administration (FDA) in August 2018 to treat dry eye syndrome. The pathway to final FDA approval involved investment by Auven Therapeutics and its subsidiary Ocular Technologies, both of which filed patent applications related to the drug and its delivery system; neither patent application named Cholkar as an inventor. Ocular was acquired by Sun Pharmaceuticals in October 2016.

The problem? Mitra apparently signed a letter waiving the university's rights in 2011,[1] claiming the work was done under the

Beyond Discovery. Jean E. Schelhorn and Joan M. Herbers, Oxford University Press. © Oxford University Press 2022. DOI: 10.1093/oso/9780197512715.003.0008

aegis of his consulting company. That waiver freed Auven to pursue the technology without a license from UMKC and for Mitra to benefit financially from the arrangement, reportedly over one million dollars.

The University filed suit in February 2019 against Mitra, Auven, and Sun Pharmaceuticals. The lawsuit alleged that Mitra knowingly violated university policy, since he did not have signatory authority to waive the university's rights to intellectual assets developed in university labs. It sought compensation for lost license revenue, among other claims. Furthermore, the lawsuit asserted that Cholkar should have been a named inventor on patent applications.

The lawsuit was settled in early 2021; UMKC is to receive US $6.45M, with $1.4 million of that going to Cholkar. Mitra has resigned from UMKC, and Cholkar now works for a pharmaceutical company.

5
Funding

Information technology that powers our phones, allows us to "google," and gets us to our destination via GPS (global positioning system) all have roots in academic research funded by government grants.[1] Similarly, National Institutes of Health (NIH) funding contributed to *all* the 210 drugs approved for use in the United States from 2010 to 2016.[2] Clearly, research funding, especially by government sources, is a primary foundation for academic commercialization.

Ownership of intellectual assets is a critical thread that should be understood for all research grants and research agreements. This chapter reviews sources of funding that support academic research, with a specific focus on ownership of the results/potential IP that stem from research funded by various sources. Recall that the academic researcher almost never "owns" products of the research, but rather develops intellectual assets that belong to the institution[3] as a condition of employment and as stipulated in institutional policy.[4] We restrict our attention here to the system in the United States and trust that those working elsewhere can find parallels to their circumstances.

We cover four major types of funding that support academic research: (1) intramural funds; (2) external grants (various sources); (3) industry-sponsored agreements; and (4) crowdfunding. The related topic of grant funding and investments directed to start-up companies is covered separately in Chapter 7.

Intramural Funds

Intramural funds are internal to the institution, and can be allocated to research through a variety of vehicles, including faculty start-up

Beyond Discovery. Jean E. Schelhorn and Joan M. Herbers, Oxford University Press. © Oxford University Press 2022. DOI: 10.1093/oso/9780197512715.003.0009

funds,[5] internal grants, salary release dollars, recognition awards, and matching funds required for external awards. These funds can be used for purposes set by the institution and often are highly flexible. They share one very important feature: any research results and intellectual property/assets derived from intramural funding sources are owned by the institution. Internal funds also include gifts. Gifts from individuals, nonprofits, or businesses are usually funneled through the development or institutional advancement office (and may require gift agreements). Note that specific outcomes cannot be stipulated by donors, although the gift can be restricted in its use. For example, a donor may provide for a student scholarship or research support in a particular area, but it cannot impose further conditions on how the gift is managed. Any attempt by a donor to do so transforms a potential gift into a sponsored agreement or contract.[6]

Intramural funds can allow faculty to pursue risky or unusual research, which in turn can produce breakthrough discoveries.[7] These funds can be deployed to support the initial stages of translational research that could produce commercializable outcomes; direct institutional support for that purpose is growing.[8] Furthermore, some institutions receive external grants to spur commercialization, which then offer internal subawards to individuals.[9] To a researcher, such a flowthrough award may seem like an institutional grant, but in fact it is subject to conditions imposed by the external funder, covered next.

External Grants

Research grants are awards from entities outside the institution that support research as outlined in a proposal/application.[10] Grants are awarded in hopes that a goal can be accomplished, but the granting organization imposes no consequences if the research fails to meet that goal.[11] Grants can be made by government agencies, foundations, and other nonprofits.[12] Researchers are adept at identifying funding opportunities and securing support for their research by submitting grant proposals. To be successful, researchers must understand the granting agency's requirements and tailor their proposals accordingly.

Academics often talk about "their" grants, but in fact such awards are made to the institution, not to individual researchers.[13] Institutions have a complete infrastructure to support grant processes including pre-award support (submission of proposals) and post-award support (administration of the grant within the institution). External grants are legal agreements between the funding sponsor and the institution.

Every funding agreement includes award terms required by the funder for acceptance of the award, such as accounting practices, animal care standards, oversight of subawards, allowable indirect costs, and project reporting. Note that terms for federal grants are nonnegotiable,[14] but some local government agencies and many nonprofits may be willing to negotiate minor terms. The terms also can include provisions for reporting inventions to responsible offices, which in turn report to the sponsor; this is really important, and many academics are unaware of their obligation to report as a condition of accepting funds. Other specifics in award terms can include who takes the lead for commercialization-relevant activities (patents development and costs, marketing, etc.), and details for sharing revenue realized from the commercialization of any intellectual assets developed with grant funding. You as Principal Investigator (PI) share responsibility with your institution to meet the award terms.

Let us focus on award terms that pertain to intellectual assets derived from U.S. federal government grants. Such grants have provisions requiring inventions be reported and that allow for commercialization as conveyed by the Bayh-Dole Act of 1980.[15] That Act allows contractors[16] to "elect title" to inventions conceived or reduced to practice[17] on federal funding. Electing title means more than just seeking ownership. An institution that elects title commits to file patent applications and to lead commercialization activity driven by the inventions. A specific timetable requires the institution to file patent application(s), market the technology, and make a good faith effort to commercialize the research results.[18] The contractor must provide the government a fully paid up, nonexclusive, world-wide license to the inventions/patents, and government rights must be noted on all relevant patents and patent applications.[19] If an institution decides to abandon a patent application, it must offer that patent back to the government. Minor differences in specifics exist across federal funding agencies, and it is the job of the contractor's tech transfer office to keep track of and comply with the exact requirements of the relevant funding agency. The researcher's responsibility is described in Box 5.1.

Passage of the landmark Bayh-Dole Act[20] spurred tremendous effort to commercialize in academic centers because for the first time they could elect title to federally funded inventions.[21] This act is credited with launching the biotech industry in the United States, and it prompted universities to establish technology transfer offices. The ensuing growth in licensing and patenting activity by research institutions has many causes, to be sure,[22] which the Bayh-Dole Act catalyzed.[23]

States and local governments are active in this arena as well. Some explicitly follow Bayh-Dole provisions, but most are silent. We actually know very little about how different states and local governments define terms for intellectual assets arising from research they support.[24] An interesting and exceedingly gray area pertains to state grants whose actual source is the federal government. These pass-through grants[25] are funded by local governments but derive from federal block grants to those governments.

Box 5.1 You start the ball rolling

You may be surprised to learn that as PI you have the first obligation in reporting requirements! A condition of *any* federal grant funding is that you must report your invention to your institution, and within two months of your report, your institution must inform the funding agency. You start the ball rolling, and we stress that you should not take this obligation lightly.

In addition to government grants, academic researchers often apply for competitively awarded support from foundations, nonprofits, trade groups and the like; this sector has become more prominent in recent decades.[26] In addition to awarding competitive grants, sometimes such an organization may approach a particular institution/researcher to conduct targeted research. Regardless, the award terms for intellectual assets from such nongovernment grants are highly variable. Some funders may only seek acknowledgment in publications; most allow the awardee institution to lead commercialization of associated discoveries; and some may expect a share of any commercialization revenues. In some cases, the funding body may even seek to take over assets if the university does not pursue commercialization.

In addition, external grant funders may impose requirements on the researchers prior to publications or other public disclosures (such as talks and posters at a conference) of results stemming from the funded research. The typical requirement is for sponsor review of all materials prepublication/disclosure, with sufficient lead time for a potential patent application filing or removal of confidential information. With such variability in requirements across funders, the PI has special responsibility to understand and comply with those conditions.[27]

Industry-Sponsored Agreements

For-profit companies provide funding to researchers for specific research or services they need. Typically, the company approaches the institution to identify a PI, but in some cases faculty can be contacted directly to consider serving as a PI. If the PI is interested, they can jointly discuss the project[28] and develop a scope of work. Negotiation of a detailed sponsored research agreement is the domain of an institutional office that you should involve early on; they are responsible for helping you develop a budget (called a quote in industry)[29] and for ensuring the developed project adheres to institutional policies. An industry-sponsored agreement is different from a grant in three key areas:

- Most important is the concept of deliverables. Deliverables are specific outcomes with an associated timeline; they might include reports, critical experiments, physical objects, computer code, clinical trial results, and so on. The institution must agree to put forth a reasonable level of effort by the PI to produce those deliverables.
- Potential IP is always considered. Typically, the sponsor seeks to obtain an option for the project results, discoveries, technologies, and the like that were created with their funding. Exercise of the option could move the sponsor into a negotiation for an exclusive or nonexclusive license agreement with the institution. Rights to background IP required to practice the project IP are also framed in the agreements.
- Dissemination of results is often negotiated. Your institution will insist on your ability to publish and use any results for educational purposes. If the sponsor balks at publication requirements, there are alternatives[30] that the PI may not find acceptable. Most often, the sponsor requires review and preapproval of any confidential information disclosure that might require patent filings. It is important that you review and accept any such terms.

Negotiations for industry-sponsored agreements can range from straightforward to protracted, depending on the specific issues that must be resolved. Furthermore, the faculty member rarely participates directly in those negotiations but is consulted about certain topics as they arise. In some cases, the institution may not be able to assure or will not accept the conditions, and a potential award may evaporate.

Industry sponsorship of basic research now outpaces that of the federal government[31] and many faculty welcome industry funding. Even so, they can be surprised at short funding periods, tight timelines, requirements for reporting, and terms which include an option to the discoveries. Industry-sponsored research projects connect you with teams that are in the market; if your work is helpful to them, they often come back for follow-on activities and funding.

An Aside: Consulting Agreements

Industry often seeks academic expertise via consulting agreements, and institutions encourage such activity.[32] Consulting agreements do not fund academic research itself but rather tap the expertise of a faculty member as the consultant. A formal agreement for consulting involves a company seeking services and an individual researcher.[33] Faculty typically must disclose such agreements and get institutional approval for a plan to manage potential conflicts of interest.[34] In addition, institutional policies may require language in the consulting agreement that stipulates the company cannot access IP rights owned by the institution. Consulting agreements nearly always require that the company owns all results and all patents derived from the consulting work. These agreements include non-disclosure language that prohibits use of confidential information outside the consulting arrangement itself.

In addition to money in your pocket, a key advantage of industry consulting is that it gives a perspective on how industry works and how it thinks about product development for markets. You can also become aware of unmet needs in the marketplace. A special form of consulting is service on corporate boards, which often includes payments.[35] Such involvement provides explicit information on market trends, product development, and competitors. Academics who serve on corporate boards or consult for industry quickly come to appreciate the market mindset and also can become motivated to pursue research needed to solve particular problems in that marketplace (again, being mindful of confidentiality requirements). Service on nonprofit boards, though not lucrative,[36] can be equally inspiring.

Special Programs to Support Consideration of Commercialization

In 2012, the National Science Foundation (NSF) instituted the Innovation Corps (I-Corps™, hereafter I-Corps) program to "enable the transformation of invention to impact," specifically to help recipients of NSF funding to catalyze commercialization. The approach has since been adopted by at least eight other federal agencies. Since its inception, I-Corps has funded more than 1,500 projects and catalyzed the formation of nearly 800 companies.[37]

I-Corps explicitly recognizes the value of linking innovators together, and thus the program funds institutions in groups (called sites and nodes, and more recently, hubs). These groups compose teams that receive specialized training. Each team includes an academic with NSF funding, grad students or postdocs from the funded lab, an entrepreneur, and a business mentor. I-Corps is focused on encouraging eventual creation of a start-up company and offers cohort-based training on topics such as defining markets and finding customers. The sites/nodes/hubs are regionally based to facilitate communication and support, and collectively they belong to the National Innovation Network. While I-Corps does not fund research per se (although it can support research to broaden market appeal), it does provide a crucial orientation for academics thinking about starting a company. Given its structure that emphasizes geographic proximity, I-Corps also helps individuals navigate and make connections into their local entrepreneurship ecosystem.

Other programs to support academic commercialization have sprung up, many funded by federal agencies.[38] The Department of Defense Advanced Research Projects Agency offers funding to academics, sometimes with an explicit expectation of commercialization by grantees. The National Center for Advancing Translational Sciences offers grants for proof of concept in the biomedical sciences, as well as resources to support translational efforts themselves. Department of Energy National Laboratories host academic scientists and engineers with their Lab-Embedded Entrepreneurship Program.[39] The NIH Catalyze program[40] funds translational research targeting heart, lung, blood, and sleep disorders. In addition to these and other federal programs, some states and local governments offer parallel opportunities, and nonprofits like the Kauffman Foundation offer grants to support systemic commercialization.

Additional opportunities are available for research-based start-up companies, which we cover in Chapter 7.

Crowdfunding

Crowdfunding is a way to ask people anywhere in the world for money. Individuals solicit help to pay bills, student groups raise money to support school trips, artists seek support for creative projects, and so on. Here we consider how crowdfunding can connect researchers with a global funding community.[41] Numerous sources exist to help individuals set up crowdfunding appeals,[42] and we refer you to them for details on designing and mounting such an effort.

Academic researchers typically ask for funds to support specific projects.[43] About 12% of scientific crowdfunding campaigns focus on developing a tool, database, software, or other methodology that might have market potential,[44] and a compelling appeal (Box 5.2) must lay out not just the commercial potential of the invention, but also how donors can help move the invention along the pipeline.[45]

Box 5.2 A successful crowdfunding project

Melissa Wilson[a] describes her crowdfunding campaign to support genetic work on the Gila monster, a charismatic lizard that lives in the deserts of North America. That appeal was highly successful and engaged 173 donors. Wilson gives practical advice for researchers and describes unexpected positive outcomes from the effort.

[a] Wilson (2019).

Crowdfunding has some distinct advantages: (1) It boosts the researcher's profile worldwide by expanding networks and attracting additional investors. (2) It serves to gauge the market for the technology; if many individuals choose to invest, that may suggest demand. (3) Donors can give precious feedback to help hone the invention, or even suggest other applications that might have larger markets. Regardless of whether the fundraising itself is successful, such investor input can be crucial for defining next steps.

You should understand how your institution handles crowdfunding projects.[46] Will the funds be deposited in a general use account, an earnings account, or a development account? Will your institution charge any fees for managing such accounts? What are the implications for intellectual property?[47] How will you comply with the regulatory environment for animal care, human subjects, and other issues? If there are deliverables (reward-based crowdfunding), who will ensure those deliverables are met? To address these issues, universities are increasingly developing policies and setting up their own platforms[48] to tap into crowdfunding interest.

A successful crowdfunding campaign must provide value to strangers. It can be as simple as supporting a cause—the value used by most nonprofits and social entrepreneurs. Some donors simply want to be early adopters. Appropriately presented, appeals that have business potential can attract donors who do not expect any return.[49] On the other hand, reward crowdfunding, in which a small gift is offered to each donor, can motivate giving.

Crowdfunders are young. Most of them are just 24 to 35 years of age. They tend to favor younger, less established investigators and otherwise are highly egalitarian in their choices.[50] They are not impressed by either lists of publications or prestigious affiliations. Rather, they invest in campaigns that are visually appealing, provide frequent updates on research progress, and offer nontraditional rewards such as a visit to the lab, an opportunity to name an animal, or acknowledgment in a future publication. Regular interaction between the fundraiser and the crowd also dramatically affects how much money is raised. Indeed, fundraising success typically is dependent on factors that have nothing to do with the science itself.[51]

Two interesting variations are crowdlending and equity crowdfunding. Crowdlending, also called peer-to-peer lending, needs little explanation. Equity crowdfunding appeals are typically mounted by start-up companies that offer shares in exchange for donations. Equity crowdfunding is subject to government regulation in many countries, including the United States.[52] Such appeals have also attracted the attention of angels and venture capitalists (VCs), which amplifies their value.[53]

Perhaps the best known and largest crowdfunding platforms are Kickstarter, GoFundMe, and Indiegogo. There are also numerous tech-intensive sites such as fundageek, fundscience and experiment, some of which have a focus on, say, health care or environmental projects.[54] In 2018, global donations to crowdfunding totaled $5.5 billion, and a further $2.5 billion was raised by equity crowdfunding.[55] Academic campaigns raised relatively small amounts per project, usually under $5,000, and the overall success rate was 66–70%.[56] Studies of crowdfunding and academic commercialization focus on start-up companies[57] and we know little about how academic researchers can exploit those platforms to commercialize inventions other than by starting a company.

Crowdfunding is expected to grow exponentially over the coming decade, with new platforms to serve niche areas appearing every year. It can be a valuable source of flexible funds for an academic inventor. While the amounts are small relative to a typical research grant, crowdfunding has an important place in the financial landscape for commercialization.

Conclusion

Nearly every dollar that funds your research comes with requirements concerning the dispositon of intellectual assets and IP from the efforts. Tremendous variability exists across sponsors with respect to ownership of intellectual assets and IP, obligations to report, and confidentiality of results. It is your responsibility to know and adhere to those requirements; offices within your institution usually have compliance/reporting roles as well. Getting the money is great—congratulations! And with it you may have a breakthrough research discovery which leads to an invention that solves a critical unmet need. Go for it!

PROFILE: Luis von Ahn

Luis von Ahn, a Guatemala native, has been affiliated with Carnegie Mellon University since 2003. He earned his MS and PhD degrees there in Computer Science and after a one-year postdoc joined the faculty. During his academic career, he received substantial funding from the National Science Foundation (including a career award), as well as a MacArthur "Genius" award. In addition, he has received recognition from both professional societies and the media.[1]

Von Ahn is best known as one of the originators of the CAPTCHA technology that provides security for internet websites. This technology, developed while he was a student, uses characters that humans can easily distinguish, but that bots cannot, to ensure a human is engaging with a particular site. Within a few years, CAPTCHA was being used 200 million times a day by thousands of websites.

In 2006 (while he was a faculty member), von Ahn and his undergraduate student invented reCAPTCHA, which leveraged the brainpower of humans across the globe who were typing in CAPTCHA letters. For the reCAPTCHA program, the words used to fool bots are actual scans from old documents that optical character recognition programs cannot read (about 30% of all words in pre-1930s documents). By using these computer-illegible words in old documents as the CAPTCHA text, von Ahn's innovation was able to scan the entire print archives of the *New York Times* within about four months. His company reCAPTCHA, which paid license fees to Carnegie Mellon, was acquired by Google in 2009, at which time the technology was being used by more than 100,000 websites and

Beyond Discovery. Jean E. Schelhorn and Joan M. Herbers, Oxford University Press. © Oxford University Press 2022. DOI: 10.1093/oso/9780197512715.003.0010

transcribing more than 40 million words per day. Along the way von Ahn sold another product, the ESP game, to Google for use in image labeling.

More recently, von Ahn and his student Severin Hacker developed the language education app Duolingo and started a company by that name. They were convinced that learning a new language is the portal to higher income, especially if that language is English, and they wanted to offer language training free to anyone. Today their app is available as freeware (with ads) or as a monthly subscription, and Duolingo has 40 million active users around the world—the most popular language app globally. The company was valued at $1.9B in late 2019. As a result of the COVID-19 pandemic, people are spending more time at home, and use of Duolingo amped up 50% in just a few months.

A few years ago von Ahn stepped away from some of his duties at Carnegie-Mellon. He retains the title Consulting Professor, which allows him to interact with colleagues and students. We expect many more innovations to arise from the fertile mind of this serial inventor and his associates!

6

Insider Advice

As a researcher, over the course of your career you can expect to gain significant insights in your field, make meaningful discoveries, and perhaps solve a significant problem. You also might develop at least one invention/technology or product/service offering that has market potential. In this chapter we offer proactive steps for you to take to raise the probability of your insights and discoveries advancing into the hands of commercialization partners. We also provide guidance on big mistakes you should avoid that could hinder commercialization.

Let's start with the two primary areas that trip up researchers inexperienced with commercialization. After researchers make one of these mistakes, they are unlikely to repeat them because the consequences can be severe.

BIG MISTAKE #1: Enabling Public Disclosure

Academic researchers need to present their work in various forms and confer with colleagues. However, if those presentations and discussions constitute enabling public disclosures and other steps are not taken prior to the disclosures, your ability to commercialize the invention/technology can evaporate. Once you fully understand this topic of public disclosure, you can factor it into the timing of scholarly dissemination. Publishing/giving talks and protecting intellectual assets can easily coexist, as long as you get the sequencing right.

Public disclosure is broadly defined as any written and/or verbal information transmitted to parties who are **outside your institution**.

Beyond Discovery. Jean E. Schelhorn and Joan M. Herbers, Oxford University Press. © Oxford University Press 2022. DOI: 10.1093/oso/9780197512715.003.0011

It includes manuscripts (when they become publicly available), poster presentations, published grant proposals,[1] progress reports for some federal grants, published abstracts, public thesis defense seminars, talks, seminars, web postings, and even dinner discussions where you elaborate on your discoveries and insights. There are two types of public disclosures: enabling and nonenabling. Enabling public disclosures are communications that include sufficient information to allow someone to practice your invention or technology. General communications that do not share details are not typically enabling public disclosures.[2] We certainly do not want to discourage you from sharing your insights in public settings. Yet we want you to have clear understanding of why unplanned enabling external public disclosures can be problematic for future commercialization. We also describe critical steps that allow public disclosures without negative consequences.

In the United States, any unprotected[3] enabling public disclosure establishes a "bar date."[4] It starts a legal clock ticking, and you have one year from the date of the enabling public disclosure to file a U.S. patent application. Thereafter you are barred from filing a U.S. patent, and hence the name. Recall from Chapter 4 that the United States is one of the very few countries that allow a patent filing to be made after public disclosure and prior to the bar date. Neither the Patent Cooperation Treaty (PCT) countries nor most of the rest of the world accept a patent application after an unprotected enabling public disclosure. A bar date is established not only by an unprotected enabling public disclosure, but also by public use, sales, or offers for sale of the products or services practicing the invention/technology.

How can you avoid these negative consequences? Two approaches can be used to circumvent damaging public disclosures.

1. Prior to any enabling public disclosure, you should connect with your commercialization office and let them know the specifics of your need to communicate with others! If a patent application is filed on the matter prior to making an enabling disclosure, *no bar date is triggered by public disclosure.*

Box 6.1 Enabling public disclosures limit filing options

Filing a patent application <u>only</u> in the United States may be acceptable (as a result of a bar date), because the United States is a large market. However, in the case of companies with significant international presence, U.S.-only patents may not offer sufficient exclusion potential to engage in licensing steps. A significant investment may be required to bring products incorporating the invention to market, and many companies may require broader international patent filings to move forward in licensing. Furthermore, having an issued U.S. patent does not stop others from practicing the subject of the U.S. patent claims in other countries where no patent protection exists. Maintaining the possibility of international filings requires you to understand public disclosure and bar dates.

---

2. Establishing a binding confidential disclosure agreement (CDA) prior to the enabling public disclosure also avoids a bar date on the matter discussed, as long as the scope of the CDA covers the disclosure and the disclosure is made only to the parties that are bound by the CDA.[5]

Unplanned or imminent public disclosures are nightmares for commercialization professionals. Not only can unplanned enabling public disclosures limit international patent protection, but imminent disclosures force quick decision making and turn patent filings into fire drills. Thus, we stress the importance of working with the teams supporting commercialization at your location well in advance of public disclosures and sharing your plans for publications and presentations that could establish bar dates. Early communication about your work allows time to determine a viable course of action. Be ready for questions on how important this planned public disclosure is. In some cases, you may elect to hold back on public disclosure in light of their advice. In other cases, they may ask you to start the processes they require to move toward consideration of filing a patent application. The first such step is usually filing an invention report (referred to in government grants and in many academic offices as an Intellectual Property Disclosure Report). The invention report (IR) is tangible documentation of your invention, and we return to this step below. Note that it serves to get action started in your institution or with your commercialization professionals, but it affords no protection in itself.[6]

A second strategy to avoid public disclosure is to execute a legally binding confidential disclosure agreement (CDA), also referred to as a nondisclosure agreement (NDA), with the specific parties with whom information exchanges are planned. A fully executed CDA (signed by appropriate officials) should be structured to cover the planned exchange of confidential information:

- Specify what information will be shared; this is known as the scope of discussions, sometimes referred to as the purpose of the CDA.
- Include all entities that will participate in discussions.
- Determine which entities will provide and which will receive the confidential information (one-way or mutual).[7]
- Identify how long the exchange of information should be allowed (the disclosure period).
- Specify how long the shared information will be held confidential (the confidentiality period).

In most cases, you must request[8] that a CDA be established and then you provide input on the first three points above. Typically, your institution sets terms for the final two conditions, based on the type of CDA that will be proposed to the other party/parties.

Note that a CDA can serve to avoid public disclosure only if the exchange is within the scope and term of the agreement: it does not provide protection for information shared otherwise. Nor does a CDA prohibit the receiving party from using shared information for an independently created invention that may have been inspired by what was shared. You should not view a CDA as a framework for collaboration, although it might be a first step. It is simply a way to avoid public disclosure within the defined scope and for the protected parties.

Exchanges between colleagues within an institution do not involve CDAs because they are part of the same organization. CDAs are rarely used between individual collaborators in different academic institutions, but disclosure to those collaborators could become problematic if they are not co-inventors. By contrast, a company or individual seeking to commercialize views a CDA as essential to further discussions; it is part of their business landscape. Therefore a company interested in working with an academic center commonly requests a CDA and likely offers its corporate template as the starting point for negotiation. Even so, the CDA is just a first step, and additional agreements may be needed to further the collaboration.

Public disclosure is perhaps the most important topic for any inventor to fully understand. *Patent and publication/enabling public disclosures can easily co-exist, but the sequence of steps is crucial, and you have much control over that sequence.* Seasoned academics with experience in commercialization are aware of the impact of unplanned public disclosure and alert the commercialization office of every planned public disclosure and associated content well before the date of disclosure. This allows early planning and joint consideration of strategy as a team (Box 6.2 gives an example for an inventor with a filed patent application).

Some institutions have processes to screen proposals, manuscripts, and abstracts/posters prior to submission to assess the

---

Box 6.2 Remain an active partner

Keep a copy of any patent filing at hand: it is your guide to what is currently in protection steps. Reviewing it periodically helps you to flag new information that is outside the scope of patent filings and to manage public disclosures. Giving the commercialization team time to review new materials affords opportunities to possibly augment patent filings or establish new filings if warranted.

impact of such disclosures, but many more have no such procedures in place. Therefore, allowing enough time for proper sequencing of patent applications and public disclosures falls squarely on you as the researcher,[9] and the earlier you engage with commercialization professionals, the better.[10]

BIG MISTAKE #2: Improper Transfer of Research Materials/Data from or to Other Institutions

Transferring materials[11] (MTA) and/or data (DTA) is often a critical need. Specific agreements are used for these transfers to insure a clear understanding of what is being transferred, the permitted use, and the length of time permission is in force. Putting such an agreement in place can be easy, and conversely, it can turn out to be very complex. The complexity of the agreements grows as (1) the importance of the transferred materials becomes known; (2) the materials are proprietary, rare, or the material is encumbered; (3) materials are coming from a commercial company and are not available commercially for purchase, and a variety of other circumstances. Recognize that, in some situations, transfers cannot move forward should the parties not reach terms. We acknowledge that transfers also occur without agreements, which can cause multiple problems.

In 2010, Stanford University provided guidance[12] that allows for nonhuman, biological materials for in vitro use to be exchanged without an MTA (see Box 6.3). This is now the norm at many institutions, and decision trees[13] may be provided at your institution to establish if an MTA is needed for a given transfer. Yet other institutions have not adopted that policy, so you must understand the stance taken by yours.

The MTA or DTA is a legally binding agreement signed by your institution and processed through the appropriate office. In the event an MTA is needed between academic institutions, streamlined versions can be deployed known as Unified Biological Material Transfer Agreements (UBMTA),[14] or custom agreements can be negotiated.[15]

Box 6.3 Human biological materials need special consideration

---

The 2010 Stanford protocols exempt many research materials from the need for an MTA, thereby allowing free movement in and out. The big exception is for human biological materials (e.g., cultured cell lines), which must be transmitted or accepted via an MTA. That proviso reflects an exceedingly complex set of ethical/ownership issues that extend all the way back to the 1950s and the story of Henrietta Lacks;[a] HeLa cells, used in research labs around the world, are derived from Mrs. Lacks's cervical cancer tumors.

[a] Skloot (2010).

These are the key points you need to consider with respect to MTA and DTA:

- You are responsible for initiating material and data transfers into and out of your lab through your institutional request processes.
- The quality of your initiation request is very helpful; provide the specifics of what is being transferred, permitted use, and term required if known; and the circumstances surrounding your decision to process the request.
- Some institutions authorize you to make decisions on whether an MTA-out is required; know the policies and use any flow charts available on your institution's website for other guidance.
- If you have moved institutions, remember to initiate an MTA/DTA to allow critical materials to be transferred to you at your new institution.
- Do not assume transfers can occur when specifying use in a grant proposal. Get a support letter indicating transfers will occur in the event the grant is awarded.
- Recognize that for industry transfers this process may be cumbersome. Sharing proprietary materials may not be viewed as

serving the company's bottom line, and execution of an MTA may get stalled in the legal department.[16]

- Consider purchasing materials if they are commercially available because purchase does not typically place restrictions on use. Even so, use of purchased materials in a new invention can introduce significant licensing issues that may hinder your ability to commercialize.
- Allocate sufficient time for negotiation of the agreements.

Now that you know about the two biggest mistakes, let's proceed to proactive steps you can take in the broader context of pursuing commercialization. By understanding and following these best practices, you can position the technology to be handled expeditiously and strategically by the professional teams that will help you.

Best Practice 1: Stay Current with the Art in Your Domain

As a researcher, you must stay current on the technical literature related to your work. However, that is a subset of the art relevant to commercialization. As we described in Chapter 4, art is also to be found in nonscholarly outlets, especially patent applications and issued patents (both in the United States and internationally). In addition to remaining current on the literature, you should also periodically look for patents related to your research.

Patents are available in domestic and worldwide patent and patent application repositories[17] that are searchable by topic, inventor name, assignee, keywords, and various legal criteria. Once you have identified a patent of interest, first examine the claims for relevance to your invention: focusing on claims allows you to screen efficiently. Then drill into the specification to understand how close the protected invention is to yours and to find nonclaimed aspects in the protected body of work. Both issued patents and patent applications have claim sets, but only issued patents have claims that have been thoroughly assessed by the patent offices and deemed enforceable.

Searching for relevant patent art helps you understand what has already been patented as well as challenges that may arise in patenting your work. The claims in an issued patent show what has been determined to be novel, nonobvious, and having a use in the patented work. The specification provides the details of how the invention is/can be practiced as well as other elements; either the claims or the specification contains potential uses/products/services/market relevant for the patented matter. Note that the specification may contain inventions and technologies that are not actually in the claims. Even so, they represent prior art that can affect your ability to patent. Through reviews of all art, you can assess the differentiation of your approach/findings relative to the closest art and the intended or potential uses in those patents. With practice, you will be able to infer where commercial companies are heading and why they are placing IP bets on particular technologies. Soon you will be reading like a pro, first by looking at the title page for issue date and then by reading claims!

Alternatively, you might search for product and service offerings that could benefit from incorporating insights or products from your research. If commercial offerings exist that could be improved with components of what you are currently developing, this line of searching could identify potential licensees for your discovery and/or funding for your work.

When does a patent application publish? Most patent applications are published 18 months from first filing; however, U.S.-only patent applications are not published until they issue.[18] Thus, there will always be patent art that exists but that you cannot see. This blind spot places a premium on watching the technical literature and associated resources as well as searching patent art regularly to stay current.[19]

If you are interested in work by a particular individual, you will surely search the online repositories for that individual's patent/patent applications. However, if the inventor has published on the topic that is the focus of the patent application, their manuscript may actually publish more quickly than the companion patent application. If you compare "matching" manuscripts/publications with published patent applications, you typically find parallel information. However, the patent application itself likely describes alternate ways to practice the invention and possible key commercial applications. Therefore, both following the literature and searching patent databases provide thorough information by which to assess your own invention.

Best Practice 2: Write a Complete and Compelling Report of Invention

In the previous section, we introduced the invention report (IR), variously called an invention disclosure, report of invention, or an Intellectual Property Disclosure Report (IPDR). Most institutions have online templates for these reports, and they are often quite streamlined. Even so, we strongly suggest you go beyond the required blanks to provide all the information needed to help your commercialization team members understand your invention, evaluate the reported invention, and speed up evaluations. Below we describe the typical criteria they will apply to your submission. Knowing the evaluation criteria can help you provide the essential information on your report of invention.

In addition to the basic information such as your name and department, you should:

- Provide the names and affiliations of all inventors. Recall that inventorship is distinct from authorship (Chapter 4).[20] Include your best estimate of the percentage of inventive contribution for each individual, decided in consultation with them, and affirm their agreement on the report or through an attached document. However, please remember that final determination of inventorship entails the practice of law and may overrule input by the scientist team, especially if claims are modified during prosecution. Inventorship could also affect future revenue sharing if the technology is licensed and revenue is realized. If the invention derives from collaboration with colleagues at another institution, an Inter-institutional agreement (IIA) will be needed for exclusive licensing to proceed.[21] Providing early input on the relative contributions/revenue-sharing information in this first report satisfies your obligations for an IIA to be established by commercialization professionals.

- Identify historic and current funding sources, including grant and contract numbers and/or internal sources. Be thorough, as all relevant funding agreements need to be assessed for obligations tied to that funding (invention reporting and rights to the work, as discussed in Chapter 5).

- Provide complete details on any public disclosures related to the invention. Include dates of disclosures, names and affiliations of individuals with whom you discussed your work, and copies of any CDAs that may have been in place to cover the discussion or exchange of information. An assessment of whether those public disclosures were enabling will likely be performed to understand whether a bar date is in effect. If an enabling public disclosure was made more than 12 months prior to your report of invention, it's a deal-stopper: thereafter, no patent filing is possible that focuses on that specific publicly disclosed information.

- Describe the unmet need addressed by your invention and/or nonobvious insight(s) you have gained and your view of potential uses/applications and relevant markets. There might be many potential applications for your technology, but at this stage focus on applications and uses that you could likely demonstrate in the near term. with the funding currently in place.[22] (Recall that for an invention to be patentable, there needs to be a use for it.) Perhaps your research did not start out to address an unmet need, but one such need occurred to you as results were generated. Descriptions of the unmet need and potential applications and markets for your work allow you and your commercialization professionals to assess markets for your potential invention. If your inventions were to be translated into products and services similar to existing offerings, consider how much better the products and services would be. You should also consider whether it might produce an evolutionary or a revolutionary change compared to what is already on the market: project the impact the adoption could have. A related consideration is whether you have a platform technology, which can serve as the basis for multiple products or services. If so, what platform of products/services would be enabled by your invention?

- Articulate details of your work that led to your invention, including experimental methods, materials, data, plots, and detailed discussion of the results. If your work moves to development of a patent application, this information and these details will form the substance of the specification, so be thorough! Provide any manuscripts submitted or in prep, and augment them with any additional details that have been developed since the manuscript was prepared. You likely have multiple experiments that illustrate the value of your invention; include details for all experiments and point out the best way to practice your invention (preferred embodiment).

- There is one additional step to take that academics may not contemplate: consider how you would get to a similar end point if you did not practice the invention you are reporting. In other words, could you solve the unmet need without using your technology?[23] This design-around exercise in many cases results in additional inventions or embodiments that can be reported. The new design-around inventions can often be more powerful and can be included in the patent application.[24] Include your thoughts on alternative approaches/materials/inventions.

- Share the results of your art searches—and if you have not yet searched the art, do it now. You understand your work and its context better than anyone else, and the searches you conduct may be more accurate than searches conducted by commercialization professionals who are seeing your invention for the first time. Your search of the art helps you differentiate your discovery from others. Even so, please recognize that your searches are first steps and that additional searches will follow and are needed.

- What is the developmental stage of your invention? How much more work will be needed to bring a product/service to market? Use the Technology Readiness Level (TRL) scale if appropriate—more on that in Chapter 7.

- Provide any information you have that validates the true need for your invention in commercial product applications and commercial markets, as well as how any assumptions you made could be tested. Provide any company contacts who could validate your views on market opportunities. If someone has reached out to you about your work from a commercial perspective, include that critical information.

- Review the inventor list again. Did any earlier work involve other contributors as a starting point for the reported invention? In such cases, additional inventors should perhaps be added to the report of invention.

- Did you use materials or data received from companies/collaborators/others? Describe how you obtained the materials. If there was an MTA/DTA in place for the materials, report all details so that relevant agreements can be assessed.[25]

- If critical experiments and results are expected soon, AND you can hold off on public disclosures for the near term, AND you do not believe your results will be scooped, a delay in potential patent filing may be warranted to allow time for development of the critical results. Point this out to the tech transfer team.

- Indicate your willingness to help further. Many academic inventors want merely to hand off the invention and return to their labs. In such cases, only relatively mature technologies stand a chance of being commercialized. While that may describe your invention, recognize that moving beyond the report of invention is typically a team sport. If you are not on that team, helping, the chances it will move to the next steps are reduced.

The report of invention can be as simple as the template your institution provides or as comprehensive as you make it. By filing a comprehensive and compelling report of invention, you provide your partners in tech transfer with the information needed to move forward expeditiously and with complete information. You have also illustrated your commitment to be a willing partner on this journey.

Best Practice 3: Understand and Support Decision Processes that Your Invention Will Pass Through

Within your institution, many inventions in addition to yours will likely be in consideration for commercialization. A comprehensive and compelling report of invention makes their assessment efficient and more robust. Furthermore, a prior relationship with the commercialization professionals greatly improves their understanding of your research area and its potential for the market. You can also facilitate their work on your behalf by understanding how they make decisions. Let us now consider a few specific evaluation criteria (EC) that will be applied to your invention, which link to the best practices shared above.

EC 1: public disclosures. This is always the first question you must answer; even if you covered the topic in your report of invention, you will be asked again! You now know the reason why this is the first criterion: an enabling public disclosure more than 12 months earlier eliminates any possibility of patent protection. We repeat: an enabling public disclosure more than one year before you submit the invention report is a showstopper!

EC 2: funding sources for the reported invention. All grants and contracts linked to your invention must be assessed to ensure institutional compliance with obligations imposed by the sponsor. Recall from Chapter 5 that U.S. federal funding imposes nonnegotiable obligations for invention reporting. If the institution decides to move toward commercialization with a federally funded invention, the institution must elect title to that invention and comply with government obligations for commercialization. Stipulations from other funders must be understood as well. For example, for some nonfederal funders, an invention report can trigger an option clause in the funding agreement, resulting in a potential licensee. Your planned use for current funding to advance the technology will inform EC 5 below.

EC 3: prior art. Comparing your technology to prior art is critical. In order to move to consideration of a patent application, the tech transfer office may need some level of confidence that the work and results constituting the invention/technology are new in the world, are nonobvious (and not merely the combination of known things), and have a potential use. If time allows, the commercialization professionals seek to assess your work relative to the art. Your help searching prior art is a prelude to their efforts and can jump-start deeper conversations beyond the words in the IR. The worst-case scenario is that your work falls squarely on top of existing prior art, which is usually a showstopper.[26]

EC 4: the potential uses/applications, leading to size and maturity of potential market(s). Potential uses/applications of the technology are always assessed, and pull medical applications/markets are by far the easiest to gauge for potential size. By contrast, inventions that could have multiple uses/applications and nonmedical platform technologies can be more difficult to evaluate and gauge concerning the size of the potential markets. Connections to companies and individuals who can validate the market analyses are especially valuable.

EC 5: if warranted, intellectual property protection strategy. If your invention has moved through the EC above, the focus then shifts to decisions on possible IP protection. Not every invention needs to be patented in order to be commercialized, and not every patented invention is commercialized. If patent applications are viewed as relevant to your invention/technology and potential market plays, there are a multitude of analyses and decision points for patent development and filing.[27]

Best Practice 4: Preparing and Prosecuting a Patent Application

The invention report you provided was a first documentation step made at a given point in time; if patent filings are sought it will be provided to the patent lawyer assigned to your case. Your early drafts of manuscripts provide crucial input, as well as additional data you may now have from new experiments. We stress this point: the commercialization professionals cannot read your mind, so you should share updated information/data as they are generated. Also, let your team know about future planned work related to the patent application's focus and associated timelines. The prior art from searches you have done or supported should also be shared with the attorney for consideration and, if relevant to the filing for conveyance, to the patent office.

The attorney preparing the patent application asks numerous questions as the case is prepared, and you should answer them quickly and completely (also see Chapter 4). The attorney's job is to develop a patent application that can withstand the rigors of prosecution and can provide the broadest protection possible, which is ultimately manifested in the scope of allowed claims. As the patent application draft nears completion, you will be asked to review it in detail. Your main job is to ensure the specification is complete and accurate, including the critical elements in the report of invention, design-around inventions, and experimental results/insights obtained since you prepared the initial IR. It is especially important to remember from Chapter 4 that after the patent application is filed, claims can be changed during prosecution, but the specification cannot. The specification and the associated priority date are locked down.[28] So, your team will be striving to strengthen the specification, consistent with the established filing strategy.

Once the patent is filed and at steps along the prosecution path, you must sign various official documents. As the patent progresses through prosecution, you will be called upon to help assess the art identified in official search reports and presented in time-sensitive office actions. While your technical insights are critical, they must be combined with legal know-how for the most powerful and accurate responses. Integrated input from you, any commercialization professionals on your team, and the patent attorney are all required—not yours alone. If you do not respond in a timely manner, the case still moves forward but without your input. As discussed in Chapter 4, patent prosecution typically proceeds through exchange of formal written documents, but in some cases you may be asked to participate in a person-to-person discussion guided by the applicant counsel.

Throughout prosecution, you as an inventor have an obligation to share with your tech transfer office any additional art you find. They in turn are obligated to share the references with the attorney to supplement the patent application and communicate it to the patent office.

After numerous communications, the patent examiner may agree to allow specific wording of amended claims and if the applicant is in agreement, at this point the patent application is "allowed." Finally, upon payment of an issue fee, the patent is issued and published.

Best Practice 5: Support Efforts to Market Intellectual Assets and Establish a Licensee

Landing a licensee is a critical step in commercialization. For the vast majority of situations, marketing is needed to identify a licensee for the next commercial steps. The first question from an entrepreneur or company shopping around and unfamiliar with the technology is, "Are there publications and additional materials that can be shared?" Thus, the key marketing action you, and you alone, can take is to publish. As we described earlier, large corporations employ technology scouts, and smaller companies are also on the lookout for technologies that would give them advantage in the marketplace. Many potential licensees first identify technologies of interest through scholarly publications as well as published patent applications and issued patents. Publish! (but remember the sequencing rules concerning public disclosure).[29] If you are contacted about your technology, by all means engage the discussion and immediately inform your commercialization partners, bringing them into the earliest discussions. By keeping them in the loop, they can gauge the potential licensee's interest, help answer questions about next steps, and ultimately take the lead in the commercialization discussions. They strive to find a licensee as quickly as possible. (Recall that if an option or license agreement is not in place within 12 to 18 months from the first filing date, international filings are less likely.)[30] As you prepare manuscripts and abstracts/posters, copy your team for their use in marketing. Your technology will be showcased on the web and will also be direct-marketed. You can help further by providing compelling visuals and text and reviewing the marketing materials for accuracy and potential commercial impact.

Other marketing strategies to consider include presenting at conferences, especially if you know industry will be represented. If your invention lends itself to at start-up platform, engage in events where potential CEOs and investors are shopping for opportunities, and learn about this path to discern your interest in a start-up role (which is covered in Chapter 7). Finally, use your network: pitch the technology at appropriate venues, and seek out industry interest and contacts at conferences. Support social media efforts that may be led by your college, university, or other entities.

Best Practice 6: Keep Your Research Moving Forward and Keep Inventing

Just because you reported an invention, you have no guarantee of finding a licensee. Indeed, having ongoing funding in place (especially federal funding) is an advantage because it signals to potential licensees that the technology continues to be advanced. Also please recognize that your first invention may not be your best and that subsequent inventions may be far more compelling! With submission of a first invention report, you as the inventor are introduced to the various commercialization resources used within your institution and in your ecosystem. In time you will also come to think about inventions in new ways—whether it is a "me too," its relevance to a large or small market, and what the relevant patent prior art reveals. You learn mistakes to avoid in public disclosures, and you start to think about what sorts of similar inventions could have larger plays in the marketplace. You also learn that this work requires personal commitment: rarely can you throw something over the wall to someone else, and magically a licensee will emerge.[31] Many academic inventors have told us that the first invention taught them the realities of reports of invention and the early required evaluation criteria. Be open to the lessons that start from your first invention report. Even if your first technology goes nowhere, your second or third may have a much better chance.

With a second invention, the academic researcher typically not only has a better understanding but also has undertaken many of the best practices above. Most important, they are ready and excited to put in the personal effort that enhances their chances of success. Serial inventors view the commercialization staff as partners rather than as service providers, and they understand they have much to gain from working together. Finally, they deeply understand and accept their role as the most important resource for landing a potential licensee who might be at the table.

Best Practice 7: A Licensee Is in Place! Best Practices to Support the Licensee

Recall from Chapter 2 that a typical license provides a grant of rights to relevant IP and to technology existing at the time of license that may not be within the IP.[32] The licensee will therefore likely expect a complete technology package transfer from the inventor team. That transfer will probably provoke additional discussions and questions to you from the licensee. Recognize that you have in-depth knowledge the licensee may need to be successful, so you should plan to convey additional information and perhaps respond multiple times. The licensee may be on a steep learning curve, or they may only need access to patent rights. In some cases, critical materials that must be transferred as a condition of the license are called out in the license agreement. Typically, we see the licensee seeking more access to the inventor in earlier stages of the license. You also may be asked to consider conducting research sponsored by the licensee or to participate in joint grant proposals (Chapter 5). Similarly, you may wish to approach the licensee directly about funding opportunities you have identified. As your institutional policies allow,[33] please help the licensee with their various needs: their success is your success. Also, keep the tech transfer office fully in the loop on all requests and your responses. Keep in mind that a license does not preclude your ability to continue that line of research, and ongoing work may result in additional funding, with additional intellectual assets that could possibly be licensed to the existing licensee. Remaining involved with the licensee (as requested and as appropriate) can be critical to moving a product toward market, and it is quite fun to watch as the inventions/technology become commercial realities.

Finally we offer some best practices for (possibly) unhappy endings.

Best Practice 8: Your Invention/Technology Does Not Survive the Evaluation Process

The EC above can lead at any point to the commercialization office deciding not to move forward, which can be frustrating to an academic researcher. We have two pieces of advice if this scenario occurs. First, don't give up. As we stressed earlier, your second or third invention can be more successful, as you learn how commercialization works and build relationships with the office.

Second, you may be able to license rights to the invention if your institution allows. This is complicated terrain, depending on funding source, institutional policies, and features of the evaluation process above. If you obtain rights to the technology, you can seek to directly license the intellectual assets to others. You might also consider starting your own company, a path outlined in Chapter 7. If the latter applies, enter that terrain with your eyes wide open.

Best Practice 9: When a License Is Terminated

Recall from Chapter 2 that most, if not all, agreements providing a grant of rights can be terminated by the licensee with about 30 days' notice. The implication of such a termination to the institution's IP portfolio can be significant. Suppose such a licensee had filed in the PCT and moved to national stage election, and then the license is terminated. That sizeable IP portfolio and related costs are back in the hands of your institution. If a subsequent licensee cannot be identified relatively quickly, your institution may decide to abandon many or all filings. Such a decision is final; you cannot re-file, nor in most cases can you easily reinstate a patent/patent application. Sometimes this turn of events can be anticipated, but often it is a surprise to the institution and the inventor. In either case, you should be prepared to support subsequent marketing efforts to find a new licensee, possibly with an accelerated timeline. If a follow-on licensee is identified, the portfolio life at license is reduced by the time used up by the previous licensee, and the licensor will typically require additional milestones, possibly from your lab, to ensure the licensed assets advance. By contrast, termination by the licensor can typically only be triggered by a breach of the license agreement (following a time period to cure that breach), which is a rarity.

Best Practice 10: When You Leave the Institution

Let's say you are an industrial employee. When you leave Company #1, you leave behind everything you created there. It is no different when you leave an academic center/research institute and move to another institution. All too often, an academic researcher views technology as theirs. To be sure, some assets are portable—federal grants are a great example.[34] You may be allowed to transfer equipment and consumables to the new institution.[35] However, IP is a tangible asset that rarely is transferred freely to another institution. For you to use IP generated at your first institution, a license to, or other arrangement with, your second institution may be required. Invention reports, patent applications, patents, and various agreements that have been cut for your materials, data, and IP and even CDAs remain at the original institution. If you need access to items, your new institution must be involved in securing rights to them. You may need to execute an MTA and perhaps a DTA when you move to a new institution. However, commercialization revenue that may be flowing from academic license agreements is unaffected: you[36] will receive revenues irrespective of where you are employed. Note that this feature of revenue sharing is a decided positive for academic researchers. In industry, recognition plans include plaques and cash awards, but these rewards rarely continue if you are no longer an employee.

An Aside: Institutions Without Commercialization Offices

Our discussion assumes that you work in an institution that has infrastructure to support commercialization. However, many academics work for two-year colleges, vocational schools, small liberal arts institutions, stand-alone research institutes, and hospitals/hospital systems, which may not have sufficient resources to set up a tech transfer office. To be sure, the principles in this book apply to all inventors. Yet for those without institutional infrastructure, it can be daunting to find support for commercialization. We offer the following suggestions:

- Engage with collaborators who work in larger institutions. We know of several inventors who have successfully patented as part of a team. In many, if not most, such situations, the collaborator's larger institution took the lead in commercialization.
- In small institutions, most research is conducted with the aid of undergraduate students. You may be able to tap into special funds that support student involvement and inventorship.[37]

- Find regional offices that support invention and entrepreneurial activity. Most states have established such offices, which typically are more oriented toward start-up relevant inventions (as we describe in Chapter 7). Even so, they can point you to legal and business resources in their ecosystem. For example, we know of regional pro-bono legal services for specific types of inventive activity (arts-focused invention, social entrepreneurs) that can write and file patent applications. The regional office can connect you with other inventors, accelerator programs, and funders as well. In Chapter 8, we describe a new initiative to support innovation and entrepreneurship among African American academic institutions in the Atlanta region.
- Be aware that some foundations (like Kauffman) offer grants to entities that in turn offer early-stage support services to inventors.
- Engage with like-minded people! Experienced inventors are often willing to support your quest for commercialization. Many localities have inventors' clubs, and there are virtual clubs online as well.
- Engage with community resources that may point to IP lawyers and others who might be willing to assist you and your institution.

We know inventors who have successfully commercialized while working in small institutions. Each has found a way to move their discoveries into products/services that have potential markets. You can too.

Conclusion

We have offered an array of best practices for your consideration focused in two areas: (1) advanced actions you can take that lead to solid articulation of your invention/technology, thereby ensuring appropriate review by commercialization professionals; and

(2) actions you should undertake to develop a positive working relationship with your commercialization office. We have highlighted show-stoppers and BIG MISTAKES to avoid along the way. If you adopt many of the best practices listed above and continue to "practice" with a second or third invention, your chances of changing the world are greatly enhanced.

The more invested you are in the commercialization process, the more you can learn from people eager to help you. We hope that you catch the inventor bug!

PROFILE: Chelsea Magin

Chelsea Magin studied Materials Science and Engineering at the University of Florida. An undergraduate internship with the Kimberly-Clark Corporation Skin Care and Treatments team introduced her to the field of skin biologics and gave her an appreciation of the industrial culture that integrates IP development with research activities. She gained experience in filing an invention report and the subsequent steps taken to file for a patent; Magin was a named inventor on three Kimberly-Clark patent applications (one of which has an international issuance).

For her doctoral degree, Magin worked with Dr. Tony Brennan, who had recently founded the start-up company Sharklet Technologies. Sharklet was inspired by the fact that sharks do not accumulate barnacles or other surface biofouling, as a result of their surface skin texture. The Brennan lab was engaged in fundamental research to understand features of shark skin that could be replicated to prevent the growth of harmful microbes that colonize both marine surfaces and medical instruments. The start-up company licensed the technology and focused further development of these materials for the health care market. As a graduate student, Magin focused on hydrogels to prevent biofouling. She developed a range of new materials and published a stream of research articles; her university applied for a patent with Magin as the lead inventor.

Magin next moved to the University of Colorado to work as a postdoctoral fellow, specializing in design and syntheses of light-responsive hydrogels to study the influence of physical cues on human cell function. There she received an NIH award and published several papers. Initially, she was planning on an academic career; however, she took a detour and joined Sharklet as an R&D engineer. Magin

Beyond Discovery. Jean E. Schelhorn and Joan M. Herbers, Oxford University Press. © Oxford University Press 2022. DOI: 10.1093/oso/9780197512715.003.0012

worked on a variety of projects and became Director of Product Development. She was co-investigator on two NIH SBIR grants and PI on a third (Phase I and Phase II). These projects resulted in multiple domestic and international patent applications. Sharklet was acquired in 2017 by a Chinese company, and at about that time Magin decided to pursue an academic career.

She currently holds a faculty position at the University of Colorado-Denver. In her own lab, Magin has attracted funding for her work from a wide variety of sources, including a sponsored research agreement with Sharklet, an NSF Career Award, and NIH grants. She keeps an eye on commercial possibilities for her work, and recently her institution filed a patent application on her biomaterial-based platforms for modeling chronic pulmonary diseases.

Her early experience in industry prompted Magin to become a serial inventor, constantly assessing her research discoveries for potential commercial applications. Just as important, she is training her own students to embrace that pathway toward societal impact. Keep an eye on her!

7

Starting a Company

> Starting a start-up is not the great mystery it seems from the
> outside. . . . Build something users love and spend less than
> you make. How hard is that?
>
> —Paul Graham

Starting a company is easy. You file business formation documents
with your local government and pay a fee, after which the company
is issued an identifying number by the government and is ready to
open its doors. After that, nothing is easy.

Why might you want to be involved in starting a company?
Academics found start-ups for two principal reasons:

1. Personal passion: the academic inventor believes deeply in
   their technology and decides to start a company to move
   it toward the market. Universities are increasingly encouraging faculty to start companies, and many accept that
   challenge.
2. Necessity: a technology does not attract a licensee, and the inventor views starting a company as the only option to move the
   product/service toward the market:
   - In most cases, academic technology is in a very early stage
     and needs to be developed further and de-risked before po-
     tential licensees show serious interest (Box 7.1).
   - In other cases, the invention is what is known as a "platform
     technology," such as a display technology or a medical de-
     livery device. Such a technology may hold considerable

Beyond Discovery. Jean E. Schelhorn and Joan M. Herbers, Oxford University Press. © Oxford University Press
2022. DOI: 10.1093/oso/9780197512715.003.0013

Box 7.1 A metaphor for many academic inventions

"The unbaked cake phenomenon: Academic researchers show up in [the] office with a metaphorical bag of flour and a cup of sugar, . . . when what investors and potential partners want is a fully baked cake."[a]

[a] Marcus (2020).

---

promise for multiple applications, but until that promise is proven in a first application, licensing interest may be extremely unlikely.

This chapter is designed primarily to help you understand the landscape for start-up success so that you can make decisions consistent with your career goals, personality, and resources (especially your time, attention, and stage of your career). Toward this end, we explore what it means and what it takes for an academic researcher to become an entrepreneur, personally launching and growing a start-up company.[1] Our secondary goal is to describe the environment of a start-up and introduce terminology used in that world. Knowing some key terms will enhance your understanding, and you may be surprised to learn the meaning of everyday words in the context of start-up companies (e.g., incubator, pivot, dilution, exit).

The nuts and bolts for start-up companies are ably described in other books,[2] articles, and websites; read them for how to get started with the mechanics. What those books rarely cover, however, are decisions academics must make, as well as personal considerations that drive those decisions. We also underscore that your research area can matter: academics who found companies are most commonly engineers and computer scientists, followed by biomedical scientists, whereas start-up companies founded by geologists, ecologists, and physicists are comparatively rare.[3]

If you are a faculty member, the most fundamental decision to make is whether you intend to leave your academic position. If you decide to resign or retire, whether to found a company based on technology created in the lab (and then licensed from the institution) or to strike out in a new direction entirely (see the Patrick Brown profile), we have little to offer that is not covered in other books on start-up companies. Rather, we focus on the scenario where you seek to continue your academic employment at some level: that is, you as the PI help to form a company and foster its growth but retain, at least in part, an academic position.

The academic PI starting a company can take on various roles (for example, the company may actually be managed by a former graduate student or postdoc).[4] Later in this chapter, we describe how decisions about the PI's role present challenges not just for the PI but also for the team running the company. Let's start with three realities:

- Commercial success, if it occurs, may be many years away. Academic research tends to be exploratory and attacks fundamental questions; in the commercial world, this is described as early-stage research. While researchers are skilled at connecting their work to societal needs (and often must propose the linkage to secure funding), a commercial use may be a difficult leap from the proposed aspirational dream. The path from early-stage bench discovery to market success requires substantial development, and many potential paths turn out to be non-viable.
- At first, you don't know how to do this. Moving early-stage research toward a market requires skills few academics have. Growing a company requires learning entirely new domains and entails a commitment that can be surprisingly onerous. Academics sometimes do not comprehend what it takes for success until they have invested years in the endeavor. We also repeat a lesson from previous chapters: you will be better the second time around.
- As a rule, you must enlist and trust partners with complementary knowledge/skills. While university inventors are certainly capable of mastering fields like product development, regulatory compliance, accounting, and sales, it is a near-vertical climb to do so on their own. For those planning to maintain a

demanding academic job as well, it is harder still. Yet, some are unwilling to trust partners to lead and advance the business: academic hubris can be a principal impediment to start-up success. Self-knowledge and introspection are key, and a PI may discover that in fact they are not the right person to advance the technology.[5]

With a legally-recognized company established, and a license to technology in hand,[6] you have entered the world of business and must make decisions based on business principles. Deciding on your role in the company is a crucial early business decision, and you can reach clarity by asking yourself these questions:

- "How much time and energy am I willing to devote to a start-up?" Many faculty simply are not interested in adding to their teaching, research, and service responsibilities, nor may they be willing to forsake the security of a system with relatively clear pathways to success. Others may be interested but seriously under-estimate the demands imposed on their time, attention, and capacity to learn in new fields. Sometimes overlooked by faculty is the substantial hassle factor of managing and reporting conflicts of interest and conflicts of commitment to the institution. For graduate students and postdocs, moving into a start-up is almost always a full-time proposition that requires long days and weeks immersed in a new environment focused on business concerns. Career stage, long-term objectives, inherent interest, tolerance of risk, need for control—all must be considered. Many an academic realizes they do not want to make such a commitment: starting a company is easy, and growing one is not.
- "Am I the right person to lead this company?" We have stressed throughout this book how commercialization culture is different from academia because we have witnessed companies founded by individuals who are not suited to that culture and who do not have the skills needed to advance the product to the market.[7] And the culture of a start-up's early phases is quite

different from the culture that emerges as the start-up matures. Taking a company from start-up through development to maturity requires adapting to multiple cultural shifts and remaining effective as business needs shift.

- "Am I willing to be coached?" We have stressed that for an academic researcher to succeed, they must submit to learning from others and finding ways to act on their business advice. Founder coachability is often a deciding factor for investors: we repeat, academic hubris is a major impediment to start-up success.

When thinking about these questions, keep in mind that the primary goal of any start-up is to advance its value proposition (VP) toward the market. The VP describes the initial or foundational product/service the company may seek to offer and differentiates it from other competitor products/services on the market: it defines the potential competitive position in the marketplace. That is, a strong value proposition aims for a large and significant market, and addresses a compelling unmet need.

Armed with a clear understanding of the VP and the self-knowledge derived from reflection on these key questions, you must decide how to staff the company. The PI can certainly assume a pivotal role as founder,[8] a decision that will affect both their academic career and the business itself.[9] In some cases, that individual serves as CEO; in others, the PI founder can identify someone with appropriate business experience to become the CEO[10] and instead assume the role of Chief Scientific Officer (CSO). Indeed, the university license granted to the start-up may actually *require* it to identify a CEO other than the PI at some point.

Perhaps most often, a PI is interested in advancing the technology, but not in running a company as CEO or CSO. Often such a company hires a graduating student or a postdoc from the lab to provide technical expertise and identifies a CEO to build the VP.[11] The PI's role devolves to assuring complete transfer of the technology, results, and insights that underpin the VP, as well as remaining available to help the fledgling company (possibly with a seat on the Board). Most importantly, the PI must cede control of the commercialization agenda to others, many of them former protégés.[12]

If you as PI found a company and assume the CEO and/or CSO role, be prepared for a substantial culture change. You will almost certainly need to rethink how you communicate your vision to a variety of audiences, ranging from potential employees to investors. Messaging must center not on the technology itself but on the company's value proposition.[13] An "elevator pitch" is essential, which distills your value proposition to about 30 seconds.[14] A compelling slide deck and/or business plan should describe paths to required funding, outline critical technical and nontechnical development leading to product/services launch, identify potential customers and sales channels, forecast sales volume, and—oh yes—have one slide devoted to the technology. You may also need to outline a strategy to protect intellectual assets if appropriate, which can be a key step in attracting investments.[15] Challenges presented by shifting from scientific audiences to business-minded colleagues and investors should not be underestimated.

Running a business means that business needs predominate. Recruiting, involving, retaining, and managing staff is different from running a lab. With few (if any) employees, you may need to outsource critical functions such as programming or testing (and develop the outsourcing contracts!). Short timelines are the norm. Patent applications must be pursued with an eye on a ticking clock. Funding is a continual concern. A chaotic and frantic environment requires you to do what needs to be done, regardless of job description or expertise. You have little (if any) backup support: when a key employee quits, a piece of critical equipment fails, or your supply chain breaks, it is you who must find a solution. And finally, as the company grows, it may outgrow you, and typically that is a good sign.

We want to briefly mention two other scenarios that interest academic researchers. Sometimes the PI is driven by interest and passion to offer a product or service to a small or niche market, which is unlikely ever to attract substantial investment from third parties. Such a "lifestyle company" usually stays small and in the hands of its founders. The other scenario involves social entrepreneurs, who offer goods and/or services through nonprofit or not-for-profit enterprises. For both lifestyle companies and social entrepreneurs, the enterprise might arise from academic research (and thus be subject to institutional policies concerning use of intellectual assets and conflicts of interest) or be unrelated to the founder's institutional responsibilities.[16] Lifestyle companies and nonprofits can be sources of great satisfaction for academic researchers, but for the rest of this chapter we focus on start-ups that have the potential to grow and reach significant markets.

The Entrepreneurial Ecosystem

Universities, governments, and industries are embedded within a web of structures labeled the Entrepreneurial Ecosystem.[17] These structures exist to foster company and job creation in their region (= tax revenues), an innovation culture that attracts human and investment capital, and product/services development. Many start-ups take advantage of components of this ecosystem.[18] We stress two realities: first, while numerous entities are available to support start-up companies, virtually all have expectations in return: there is no free lunch.[19] Second, these entities function primarily as funders, guides, mentors, and cheerleaders, leaving the hard work to you and the start-up team.

Academic institutions increasingly encourage researchers to launch start-up companies as a means to commercialize intellectual assets.[20] The commercialization office exists in part to facilitate launches, and it offers training and education for academic researchers as part of its mission. Faculty-led start-ups likely must license intellectual assets from the university[21] and may be offered quick standard agreements (express licenses).[22] Most start-up companies are asked to provide equity[23] to the licensor as a term within the license.

If you are to retain an affiliation with your academic institution as well as the start-up, you must comply with a suite of institutional policies, including those concerning conflicts of interest and conflicts of commitment. A faculty member who becomes CEO or CSO, or who receives compensation,[24] must disclose such conflicts and develop an approved plan to manage them.[25] Other policies govern the use of university space for housing start-up companies. Many universities explicitly disallow use of research labs,[26] whereas others regulate the square footage and rental fees for a start-up company; start-ups can quickly outgrow those restrictions and need to find alternative space. There also may be institutional policies concerning how licensee start-up companies can apply for and manage grant funding.[27] Clearly, you must understand how your institution regulates involvement with start-up companies.

Many large universities have established affiliated research parks and incubators, where start-up companies are chosen via a competitive process to be awarded space. Each such incubator has its own application rules, as well as conditions for accepting the award. There may be a strict timetable for achieving product development benchmarks, deliverables tied to keeping your berth, and a finite expectation for tenancy. Furthermore, many incubators require equity in the start-up company itself. Incubators play key roles in guiding the company's development by offering training, shared facilities, supportive business processes, access to advisors and proximity to like-minded entrepreneurs. Incubators are themselves part of regional and national networks, including connections with funders and IP experts.[28]

A different model for supporting young companies is accelerator (boot camp) training.[29] Accelerators are short-term series of learning modules that are cohort-based, which means participants learn from each other as well as from the instructors. Furthermore, they focus on the entire start-up team, not just the founder. These tend to be regional, and many offer seed funding to the start-up in exchange for equity. Accelerators are time-intensive, cramming many sessions within a short timeframe (e.g., 3 months), and often require travel to a training site. Accelerators, while open to all, can be highly competitive. Many are discipline-specific, including IT-focused and biotech accelerators. In addition to content instruction and coaching, accelerators offer important access to networks of other entrepreneurs, funders, and potential business partners. Increasingly, they serve a credentialing function: graduates of accelerator programs may be more attractive to funders.

In Chapter 5, we described the array of funding opportunities available to inventors prior to company formation. Many of those opportunities are available to start-ups, and some institutions offer funding and recognition to their affiliated start-up companies[30] as well. Furthermore, many of those early funding sources (e.g., I-Corps) provide *nondilutive* funding: there is no expectation of equity in the company, and therefore the funding does not dilute the company's value to existing owners. These seed funds may get you started, but they represent just a drop in the bucket of the money you will need. While they serve a critical need at the outset, they cannot sustain a company over time.

Government funding agencies that award nondilutive funding range from national to regional agencies, each with its own rules. In the United States, federal agencies offer two grants of special interest to small companies,[31] including start-ups. Small Business Innovation Research (SBIR) and Small Business Technology Transfer (STTR) grants are funded by the Department of Defense, NSF, NIH, the U.S. Department of Agriculture, and other agencies[32] to help small companies develop and bring technologies to market successfully.

SBIR/STTR grants can only be submitted by the company, which must be based in the United States and primarily owned by U.S. citizens/residents. The programs differ in how budgets must be structured and how the work is done. For SBIR grants, up to 30% of the grant funds can be spent on research or other services from contractors; the company itself must do most of the research and development work. By contrast, STTR grants require that a nonprofit research partner be included in the proposal, and up to 60% of the funds can be devoted to the nonprofit organization/research partners/contractor.[33] For both programs, the small company and the contractors can request indirect fees (which can be used to cover appropriate indirect costs) and in some cases, a capped fee that has few restrictions (think covering IP costs . . .). For the SBIR program, the PI must be employed (in meaningful part) by the company, with strict policies concerning conflict of commitment; for the STTR program, the nonprofit research partner can provide the Principal Investigator/Program Director (PI/PD)[34] for the grant, and the company can have a PI/PD as well. Like most grant programs, these have focus areas for funding, and you may have to search across agencies to identify one that fits your company.

SBIR and STTR grants are phased as a function of the start-up's developmental stage.[35] Phase I is a seed-grant program designed to advance the merit, feasibility, and commercial potential of early-stage technologies (proof-of-concept); Phase II grants are awarded to companies that have completed a Phase I project and demonstrated commercial viability;[36] and Phase III recognition provides follow-up support from the agency rather than dollars. These programs offer substantial grants, and have moderate funding rates (Table 7.1). Obtaining an SBIR/ STTR grant can be an important step in advancing the VP for any start-up. However, these grants are quite competitive, and so you must decide if applying for one is a good business strategy.

Table 7.1 Characteristics of the SBIR and STTR programs, from the 2017 annual report[a]

	SBIR	STTR
Federal agencies involved	11	5
Total Awards (USD)	$2,673,410,381	$368,524,326
Phase I		
Proposals Received	19,018	2820
No. of Awards	3223	613
Success Rate	17%	22%
Average Award Size	$162,986	$179,271
Phase II		
Proposals Received	3145	414
No. of Awards	1871	234
Success Rate	60%	56%
Average Award Size	$747,959	$738,993

[a] https:// www.sbir.gov/ awards/ annual-reports

Additional federal programs like the Biomedical Advanced Research and Development Authority (BARDA)[37] focus on market readiness and can be useful for start-ups that meet their requirements. For some programs, companies must identify their Technology Readiness Level (TRL), a nine-point scale to describe a technology's maturity; developed at NASA, the TRL scale is widely used as a criterion for Department of Defense (DOD) contracts and has analogs in the European Union.[38] Again, programs differ in their areas of interest, so you may have to search to find one that targets products/services into a market you wish to enter.

State and local governments also fund start-up companies. Indeed, 15 states offer matching funds to federal SBIR/STTR awards.[39] Because job creation is an important mandate for states, counties, and cities, many offer additional help to small businesses in the form of grants, low-interest loans, tax abatements, training, and the like. When you investigate your local ecosystem, tune into the *quid pro quo* expected from local governments: some programs require a commitment to maintain a physical presence in the region, while others tie funding to the number of jobs and payroll the company expects to create (which in turn generate tax revenues). The funding is nondilutive, but there may be other strings attached.

Finally, the private sector plays a crucial role in the entrepreneurial ecosystem, and here we concentrate on groups that invest in start-ups. Most start-ups are initiated with founder cash, as well as funding from friends and families and, increasingly, crowdfunding. These private sources of money can provide early support, but rarely become long-term solutions for growing a company. During early development, start-ups can tap into sources described above; later, when the technology is matured and the value proposition has solidified, young companies may be in a position to solicit funds from two groups of investors, angels and venture capitalists.[40] Making the transition from early-stage funding sources to seeking support from investors represents a huge challenge for any start-up company.

Both angels and venture capitalists (VC) invest in start-ups. A key distinction is that angels invest their own money, while venture capitalists typically invest other people's funds. Angels can be individuals, but often they are organized entities, and many are affiliated with the Angel Capital Association, a national umbrella organization. Angels are motivated by a desire to help entrepreneurs, as well as by the opportunity to make money. Angels provide seed funding, especially for earlier-stage, often premarket, companies, and their investments tend to be small. Many are entrepreneurs themselves and are willing to provide help and encouragement to the companies they fund.

By contrast, VCs are professional managers of time-sensitive funds,[41] which pool contributions from numerous individual investors. VCs have deeper pockets than angels and tend to invest at a somewhat later stage, often after the company has entered the market. Furthermore, as professional managers, they usually take an active role advising/directing companies in which they invest. Because investments are large (often reaching millions of dollars), a VC conducts intensive diligence, monitors investments closely, and exerts influence to ensure success for enterprises they fund.

Both angels and venture capitalists hear pitches from numerous companies; they make decisions about investing based on the value proposition, the technology maturity, the time to profitability, and most importantly, their assessment of the start-up team.[42] This last point cannot be overstressed: a great idea pitched by a dysfunctional team (or one that is not coachable) has poor prospects, whereas a weaker idea pitched by a sterling team can be attractive. Angels and VCs invest in teams as well as products. Finally, these groups usually do not invest alone but prefer to join after others have invested as well. Thus, your company may need a commitment from a lead investor before it is attractive to others.

Angels and VCs provide dilutive funding, meaning they expect equity in the company.[43] In addition, the primary outcome investors desire is an "exit." Angels and VCs invest with the expectation that your start-up company will be acquired by a larger firm, thereby generating enough cash to pay investors with a large return on the investment.[44] Because start-ups carry high risk, these investors seek high returns on invested capital, which an exit affords. Indeed, a key component of a pitch to these sorts of investors is to identify possible corporations that might provide that exit[45] as well as comparable companies that have successfully exited and what returns were realized. So here's the catch: if you want investment capital, you as the inventor must be willing and plan for your company to be acquired.

A final group in the private sector that has keen interest in academic start-ups is industry itself. Large companies monitor the progress of start-up companies and keep tabs on their intellectual assets, even if they have decided not to license those assets directly from the university. Such a company may monitor the technology for maturation/advancement; it might invest in the start-up[46] or it might seek a seat on the Board. At a later point, the large company may even acquire the start-up.[47] The major factor affecting a large company's interest in the start-up is its assessment of risk. Early-stage technologies are inherently risky, and start-up companies assume all the risk at the outset; those that survive and thrive demonstrate that the risk has been abated and become increasingly attractive to large companies.

The transition to seeking investment capital requires new mindsets and behaviors for academic inventors. You not only need a solid business plan and a slick presentation, but also must become conversant with cap tables and due diligence, to name just two new terms. Investors make decisions based on myriad factors as they assess the likelihood of your company's ultimate success. A good product, significant market, skilled start-up team, and willingness to be coached all make your company more attractive. This is serious business, and you must take it seriously.

The entrepreneurial ecosystem encompasses many entities that support start-ups, and the key word is "support." Company personnel retain full responsibilities to write code, develop the product, submit SBIR/STTR proposals, pitch to investors, attend training, sell, market, file tax returns . . . and make the company profitable. Your goal of addressing unmet societal needs must be tied to making money in the market. Academic metrics (other than publications pertinent to the technology) are simply not relevant!

Some Inconvenient Truths

Truth 1: This is hard work. Most start-ups fail,[48] and even successful start-ups can take 10 years or more to become profitable. If you remain in your academic position, you have to manage conflicts of interest and conflicts of commitment. The company may need to pivot, so that the final product and market may bear little resemblance to the original vision. Your second start-up company has a much higher chance of success than your first. You must be coachable and take advice rather than give it. You as the inventor must be willing to let go.

If you understand and accept the contours of this landscape, and then commit to launching a company that will thrive, all within the context of self-reflection, you have a reasonable chance of success. Start-up companies are inherently fragile; the top three causes of failure[49] are insufficient market need, insufficient funding, and a nonfunctional or suboptimal team. Thus, tracking the market (and your competitors), fundraising, and developing a strong business team and culture should be top priorities.

Truth 2: Much of the support you have received within the academic world disappears when you work outside its walls. Previously, your institution provided staff support, whether in your department, in sponsored programs, or in tech transfer; paying many of the bills was not your responsibility. However, when you shift into a start-up, everything falls in the lap of the company, from submission of grant applications to human resource functions. If you are fortunate to be awarded a berth in an incubator, you can take advantage of some shared support (such as copy machines and receptionists to answer the phone).[50] Let's drill into one such responsibility: IP management (remember Chapter 4?).

Like every other aspect of the start-up culture, managing IP is driven by business decisions—which must be informed by technical and legal know-how. In our experience, the jump to IP portfolio management is difficult, as start-ups struggle to prioritize commercial need for IP protection while facing ever-escalating costs. Of particular importance to start-ups is the question of whether the product or service you plan to offer has potential to infringe the patent(s) of others. Recall from Chapter 4 that patent offices do not offer any opinions about your ability to *practice* your issued patents; this is the responsibility of the business.[51] So bear in mind that as the start-up matures, managing IP becomes more a business strategy than a technical process. Furthermore, it is of intense interest to potential investors and can become a deciding factor in their decisions.

Truth 3: The chaotic all-hands-on-deck culture of a fledgling start-up morphs as the company matures and moves toward the market. Along the way, your company must navigate phases of fundraising from multiple sources. Markets can shift, and you may need to pivot to a different unmet need for which your technology is appropriate. Early customers will provide valuable feedback to help you hone your value proposition. Running a business means that staff may come and go: people who work in your company are not your students! Your own ability to commit time and attention can vary over the years. And if you can no longer fulfill the managerial functions (because life happens), your company may collapse.

Many (probably most) founders leave the company as it grows.[52] Some realize they no longer want to allocate the time and attention needed of a CEO/CSO; others find they do not have the personality traits to successfully lead a nonacademic enterprise. A worst-case scenario, not uncommon, is that the board recommends a founder separate from the company. Letting go or being pushed out is a bitter pill indeed, but may be necessary if your original invention is to reach the market and the company is to thrive.

Conclusion

Starting a company is a heady prospect and entirely different from the familiar academic environment. For early-stage technologies, it may be the best (or only) option. There are numerous resources to help you succeed, but they can do so only if you commit to meeting the intense needs of a young company. Short timelines, flat administrative structures, and an extremely steep learning curve present challenges that few academics anticipate. As the company matures, you must continue to adapt and acquire new skills. But having the fruits of your research reach and succeed in the market— now, *that's* impact!

PROFILE: Tish Scolnik

Natasha (Tish) Scolnik was a mechanical engineering student at the Massachusetts Institute of Technology (MIT) when she took a seminar course on wheelchair design for developing countries. Her instructor challenged the class to rethink wheelchairs for people needing to navigate rough terrain and long distances to work or school. Scolnik and her student colleagues examined those use criteria and quickly learned that conventional wheelchairs are heavy, hard to navigate, and expensive to fix. They decided to start from scratch, with a special goal of meeting the unmet needs of the disabled in the developing world.

Thereafter, Scolnik spent an internship in Tanzania, working with nongovernment organizations (NGOs) and wheelchair manufacturers. When she returned to MIT, Scolnik continued to work with classmates on a prototype wheelchair that addressed third world market requirements: it had to be light, able to traverse difficult terrain, and easy to fix. The team recruited wheelchair users to try out their prototypes, and by 2012 they had a workable model. They realized their product would be attractive in additional markets as well (developed countries). They won the MIT MassChallenge competition, and the prize provided capital to launch a start-up company.

Scolnik and classmate Mario Bollini founded Global Research and Innovation Technology, Inc. (GRIT)[1] to further develop and market their Freedom Chair. It is a revolutionary design and improvement for an established market: the Freedom Chair has three wheels and uses levers at chest height to propel the chair and to provide steering control, which takes much less energy. Made with standard bicycle parts (a supply chain shift), the Freedom Chair is

Beyond Discovery. Jean E. Schelhorn and Joan M. Herbers, Oxford University Press. © Oxford University Press 2022. DOI: 10.1093/oso/9780197512715.003.0014

lightweight, easy to take apart, and simple to repair. The Freedom Chair has scaled mountains, taken riders for miles-long hikes, and provided mobility to thousands who thought they would never be able to get around singlehandedly. GRIT maintains close ties with its customers through a Facebook page and active blog, and it continuously uses feedback to improve design features. The company has also developed partnerships with the Multiple Sclerosis Society and the Spartan Race, as well as leaders of the wheelchair-bound community.

The inventor team filed for patents, and one patent has issued (US 8,844,959).[2] A major market adoption milestone was approval from the U.S. Office of Veterans Affairs to market the Freedom Chair to military veterans. Scolnik as CEO has secured several rounds of angel funding, providing capital to mature the product and company and to reach new markets. GRIT remains committed to providing products to developing countries and works with NGOs to distribute the Freedom Chair in several countries. In the United States, they are experiencing continued growth and sales. In 2019 Scolnik was honored as the inaugural winner of the Cleary Insurance Boston Business Risk Award.

8
The Equity Imperative

When asked to name an inventor, most Americans think of Thomas Edison rather than George Washington Carver or Ada Lovelace. Edison's inventions included the incandescent light bulb and the phonograph, while Carver introduced crop rotation to agriculture and Lovelace developed and published the first computer algorithm. All three made important contributions that had lasting societal impact.

In this chapter we explore what the above hints at: commercialization presents additional challenges for individuals who are not stereotypical inventors—that is, who are not white/Asian men. In the United States, societal movements such as Black Lives Matter and the Women's March are shining light on structural inequities that disadvantage women and minorities. The world of commercialization is no different. In this chapter we briefly describe representation of women, blacks, Latinx, and indigenous inventors in academia, and then delve into some causal factors that disadvantage women and minorities in tech transfer.[1] We end by describing efforts that are redressing the imbalance.

This chapter more than any other interprets the work of social scientists and brings in our personal experiences along the way. Most research on inequities in the world of commercialization focuses on start-up businesses,[2] and we know much less about how gender and ethnicity affect industrial funding, invention disclosure activity, licensing deals, and the like. Even so, the available information consistently implicates similar patterns and causal factors throughout the complex network of research translation.

Beyond Discovery. Jean E. Schelhorn and Joan M. Herbers, Oxford University Press. © Oxford University Press 2022. DOI: 10.1093/oso/9780197512715.003.0015

Patterns of Representation

Scientists tend to be male and white/Asian.[3] The "leaky pipeline" metaphor documents how girls/women are lost from the ranks of potential scientists as they proceed through the education and training process.[4] Despite substantial progress in educational achievement,[5] the ranks of professional scientists continue to be male-dominated, even in disciplines like biology for which women achieved parity among degree recipients a decade ago.[6] In some disciplines, notably computer science, degrees to women actually declined in recent years. The net result is that women remain in the minority on science faculties, ranging from about 30% in the life sciences to under 10% in physics and most engineering specialties.[7] Women in industry are similarly underrepresented.[8] Furthermore, they hold far fewer powerful positions among campus leaders.[9]

One particular gender gap concerns us here: academic women have fewer ties to industry than men, and male faculty are much more likely to receive support from industrial sponsors.[10] This disparity cannot reflect research quality because women are awarded competitive federal grants at par with their representation. The gender gap in industrial funding starts early: female graduate students are less likely to be supported on industrial grants and contracts.[11] Furthermore, women working in industry move into academic jobs far less often than do men.[12] The net result of these factors is that academic women are less familiar with industry, develop fewer collaborations with industrial colleagues, and attend fewer conferences that focus on industry concerns.

Gender gaps are evident in tech transfer as well. Invention disclosures within universities are male-dominated, and one study[13] that controlled for potentially confounding factors like discipline, specialty, and rank found that male science faculty were 43% more likely to disclose inventions than women.[14] Data from the U.S. Patent and Trademark Office (USPTO) show that women are profoundly underrepresented among patent holders in general,[15] and data from other countries show similar patterns.[16] Notably, academic women are more likely to patent than their counterparts working for industry.[17]

The exception to a patent gender gap lies in the biotech industry.[18] There, women are slightly *more* likely to patent, especially in geographic hubs like Boston and San Diego. Biotech as a discipline produces PhD-level scientists at gender parity, and the industrial sector is characterized by a mix of start-ups, small companies, and large pharmaceutical firms. Small companies tend to have a flat administrative structure, highly flexible roles, and organized networking,[19] all of which are attractive for women.

Similarly, holders of SBIR grants are predominantly male,[20] as are participants in I-Corps programs.[21] Women-led initiatives find fewer berths in accelerators and incubators,[22] and they attract far less start-up capital, especially from angels and venture capitalists.[23] Women are underrepresented on corporate boards for technology companies as well.[24]

All these data are troubling, and we know even less about how minority (non-Asian) academics commercialize.[25] Nationwide, whites and Asian Americans compose 89% of the science and engineering workforce. Hispanics are clustered in the social sciences, and blacks have (relatively) strong representation in the computing sciences. Among these minorities, women remain underrepresented as well, meaning that women of color represent a tiny fraction of professional scientists and engineers. Research-intensive universities where most commercialization occurs have fewer still: the total for non-Asian minorities rarely exceeds 5% (but see Box 8.1).[26]

Box 8.1 At the intersection of gender and race

For two examples of successful academic inventors who are also women of color, see the stories of physicist Shirley Ann Jackson[a] and biologist Lydia Villa-Kormoroff.[b]

[a] https://president.rpi.edu/president-biography
[b] https://amysmartgirls.com/20for2020-dr-78d197fdbf3c

The small numbers problem means that academic STEM (science, technology, engineering, and mathematics) minorities with intellectual assets that might be commercialized are rare and virtually unstudied.[27] We do know that SBIR grants funded by the NIH are rarely given to minorities (only 2% to Hispanics and 0.3% to blacks),[28] and these groups patent at low rates as well.[29] To gain additional insight, we must use knowledge gleaned from broader studies of minority entrepreneurship.

Causes of Underparticipation in Commercialization

It is useful to frame academic commercialization in terms of supply and demand.[30] Supply factors limit interest and involvement in commercialization, while demand factors hinder access to resources needed for success.

Supply factors limiting women's commercialization derive from gendered psychological and sociological factors.[31] In fact, men and women have similar entrepreneurial bents, but men are much more likely to actualize their intentions.[32] Women's hesitation derives from several sources. First, they have low confidence in their skills needed for an unfamiliar activity; far more often than men, they believe that prior experience is necessary before they can succeed. Second, women are far less likely to envision themselves as capable of moving into translational arenas.[33] Third, risk-taking is gendered.[34] That is, women's view of risk-taking is overwhelmingly weighted toward the probability of failure, whereas men's is weighted toward the probability of success.[35] Gendered attitudes toward risk have two additional consequences. For women, early failures deeply discourage further activity compared to men, and women tend not to be serial entrepreneurs.[36] On the other hand, sensitivity to risk means that women are better equipped to think strategically about their strengths and weaknesses: those that do venture into commercialization are better at identifying skill sets needed to complement their own.

Women benefit by having role models. In addition, a vigorous network that supports commercialization activity and provides mentoring is essential to women's involvement.[37] Yet we know that women scientists have shallower and more transient networks than men.[38] They tend to have fewer collaborators and go to fewer professional conferences; they do not retain collaborators in their networks for as long. Furthermore, they are far less likely to have industrial contacts in their networks, which can limit their options for industrial funding and license deals. Clearly, developing robust networks that include industrial colleagues is key to women's involvement in commercialization.[39]

Finally, women tend not to respond to inducements that center on money.[40] Commercialization offices like to highlight potential fiscal rewards, but that is not a sufficiently powerful incentive to overcome women's aversion, especially when they are successful with traditional funding sources like federal grants. Universities seeking to increase commercialization by women scientists will gain by reframing the benefits of those activities.[41]

How supply factors might limit commercialization by minority academics is virtually unexplored.[42] To be sure, familiarity is important: knowing an entrepreneur encourages entrepreneurship behavior.[43] Further, there are important differences among ethnic groups in financial risk tolerance.[44] And that's about the sum of what we know: commercialization behavior by minority STEM researchers remains badly understudied.

Demand factors that differentially affect women and minorities are systemic features of universities, the tech transfer world, and the realm of start-up companies; the single most important factor is unconscious bias (Box 8.2).[45]

A second strong influence on commercialization behavior is academic culture.[46] Women are acute observers of department and institutional values, and tend to structure their work to align with them. Entire disciplines (e.g., physics) devalue industrial support in favor of federal grants, and even those that are heavily linked to industry (engineering, biotechnology) may prioritize traditional funding streams. That value structure discourages faculty, especially those

---

Box 8.2 What is unconscious bias?

Unconscious bias derives from associations that we as human beings have with concepts of who is a scientist, who is an inventor, and who is an entrepreneur. These mental concepts are based on our experience and cultural norms and, most often, conjure up males who are white or Asian. Thus, when we think about commercialization, *all of us,* our first thoughts tend to be about men, not women or blacks.[a] Unconscious bias strongly affects the way we think and behave, and counteracting it is possible.[b] Many scientists and engineers think they are immune from unconscious bias because they have been trained to be open-minded to all ideas. Yet scientists, too, display unconscious bias:[c] no amount of scientific training can erase societal messages received since early childhood. Awareness of bias and strategies to circumvent them are essential to erase inequities built into our institutions and systems.[d]

[a] Many women have unconscious bias against women, and many minority individuals similarly have unconscious bias against other minorities.

[b] Numerous books, blog posts, and articles give best practices, and you can easily find a consultant to provide training. The landmark study (Gouldin and Rouse 2000) focused on orchestras and showed that blind auditions resulted in many more women being hired. Today musicians audition behind a screen without their shoes (because the tapping of heels could clue gender).

[c] Moss-Racusin et al. (2012) is the seminar paper on this topic.

[d] Stewart and Valian (2018); Laursen and Austin (2020).

---

who are risk-averse, from engaging in commercialization activity.[47] The second and closely related component of department culture is its reward system, including salary raises, teaching assignments, research space, grant dollars, access to graduate students, and support for collaborative activities. To be sure, both men and women structure their activities to align with the prevailing reward system, but women often lack access to invisible networks of power and must rely on written codes.[48] A reward system unaligned with commercialization is unlikely to produce commercialization behavior, especially among women.

Women and minorities also experience a disproportionate share of service responsibilities.[49] In addition to being asked to do more committee work,[50] women and minority science faculty tend to assume more of the "invisible work," such as talking with students who drop by, informal mentoring, and (for women) academic housekeeping like taking notes at committee meetings.[51] Well-meaning administrators who want to include women and minorities in decisions often overburden the few, who can find it hard to refuse. The net result is that women and minority faculty have far less discretionary time than do their white male colleagues. In short, they are busier than their majority colleagues and have less bandwidth for commercialization activities (especially in the last year, see Box 8.3).

Women who do pursue commercialization may find themselves stymied by institutional structures. Competition for internal accelerator awards is male-biased, and commercialization staff members can exhibit unconscious bias against women inventors.[52] University-affiliated incubators provide less space to women inventors as well.[53] Those patterns contribute to gender gaps in patenting, industry connections, and start-up company foundation. Without vigilant oversight of access to resources designed to encourage commercialization, institutions run the risk of discouraging their female

---

Box 8.3 Constraints on men and women during the pandemic

The COVID-19 pandemic has exacerbated these patterns, with women bearing more of the added responsibilities of children being schooled at home.[a] Women have published less, reported increased workloads and less time for research, as well as other negative effects.[b] Simple interventions can have substantial impact and ameliorate these effects.[c]

[a] Kramer (2020); Myers et al.(2020); Servo et al. (2020); Deryugina et al. (2021).
[b] Andersen et al. (2020); Higginbotham and Dahlberg (2021).
[c] Witteman et al. (2021); Misra et al. (2021); Fulweiler et al. (2021).

inventors. *No parallel studies exist for minority faculty*, and we suspect they are disadvantaged as well.

Founders who start companies face further gender- and ethnicity-based differentiation of opportunity. In addition to disparities in SBIR and STTR grants,[54] women and minorities also rely on personal funds, support from family members, and lines of credit more often to fund the business.[55] They pitch less frequently to angels/venture capitalists, and they are less successful when they do.[56] Investors are sharply influenced by unconscious bias: they have a mental image of successful founders as male and either white or Asian.[57] This leads them to ask different questions of women, to dive more deeply into the financials, and to focus on the potential for failure rather than the potential for success.[58] Lack of diversity among the funders themselves can be an obstacle, and inventors presenting products and services that do not resonate with white males are at a serious disadvantage.[59] Thereafter, women-led companies continue to face disparities, such as initial public offerings (IPOs) that exhibit gender gaps in valuation.[60] Overall then, the playing field for women and minorities is deeply uneven, with women of color facing even more challenges.[61]

Leveling the Playing Field

In Chapter 3 we described how an increasing emphasis on translational research has been reinforced by national organizations.[62] Inclusion of explicit language in tenure and promotion materials is an important step to encourage women and minority faculty to consider commercialization. Furthermore, specialized institutional programs that address gender gaps in commercialization[63] have sprung up, including REACH for Commercialization at Ohio State[64] and the Women in Innovation and Technology program at Washington University-St. Louis.[65] Commercialization officers, who play key roles in deciding which technologies to promote,[66] can be trained in unconscious bias, and professional societies likewise are active in promoting inclusivity.[67]

The new platform of crowdfunding, whereby companies pitch online for start-up capital and receive microinvestments from many individuals, is inherently more equitable than other sources.[68] A study of Kickstarter data showed that women represented 35% of the project leaders and 44% of the investors.[69] Furthermore, women-led companies (of which few were tech-based) had higher levels of success than the men-led companies. As we described in Chapter 5, crowdfunding can fill gaps in traditional funding streams, especially for young start-up companies.

The concept of intentional investing has achieved considerable traction.[70] The undisputed leader of the concept is Golden Seeds, an angel group that invests only in start-ups that have women in the C-Suite.[71] This fundamental philosophy is based on research showing that companies with women executives have better business processes and generate higher profits than those run by all-male teams. Started in 2005, Golden Seeds has expanded to a national consortium of several hundred groups. Collectively, they have invested more than $150M in women-led companies, started an affiliated venture capital fund, and developed training modules for investors. Angel groups themselves are increasingly diverse: today 20% of all angels are women,[72] and more than 20% of all angel-funded companies are led by women. Those data stand in sharp contrast to venture capitalists, of whom less than 10% are women.

In addition, government programs (especially in the Small Business Administration [SBA] and the Minority Business Development Agency of the Department of Commerce) and numerous other entities provide targeted funding for start-up companies owned by women and minorities. The SBA in particular has been active in research on women and minority-owned companies, and is especially interested in the STEM sector that fuels economic growth.[73]

Specialty incubators and accelerators for women and minority-led companies have become important vehicles for intentional investing.[74] Most of these support businesses and entrepreneurs regardless of sector, and many are geographically based. Incubators and accelerators that focus on the STEM sector, however, tend not

---

Box 8.4 An accelerator for women in STEM

The STEM2Market accelerator specifically guides women STEM entrepreneurs[a] and also trains funders in intentional investing techniques. Targeted recruitment allowed them to reach a diverse audience, and more than 50% of the accelerator participants have been women of color.

[a] Stemtomarket.org

---

to provide specific support for underrepresented groups (but see Box 8.4).

The mission of the Kauffman Foundation of Kansas City is to support entrepreneurship broadly, and its Inclusion Challenge provides funds to organizations that find new ways to engage women and minority entrepreneurs.[75] Grantees for the Kauffman Inclusion Challenge include universities and community-based consortia that address both the supply-side and the demand-side factors that have historically disadvantaged women and minorities. While the program does not specifically target STEM disciplines, several of its most recent grantees are science-based. Private-sector innovation is now starting (Box 8.5) to address these gaps as well.

Box 8.5 A program for black scientists and engineers

Pledges announced in January 2021 by Apple Computer and the utility Southern Company will provide $25M to support the Propel Center[a] in Atlanta, Georgia. This innovation campus will serve four historically black colleges and universities (HBCUs), with a specific focus on STEM entrepreneurship.

[a] https://edfarm.org/programs/propel-center

Conclusion

Like many of our systems imbued with structural inequities, the world of commercialization disadvantages women and (non-Asian) minorities. By understanding the nature and effects of systemic inequities, we are moving from the decades-old attitude of "fix-the-women" or "fix the minority" to *fix the system*. Institutions that wish to foster a commercialization agenda should ensure that their processes and policies for technology transfer are aligned with institutional equity ideals. Further, tracking internal data by gender and ethnicity on disclosures, licenses, patent applications, access to incubator space, and so on is imperative. Only in that way can an institution evaluate gaps and then develop procedures to ensure every inventor has access to the same opportunities and support for commercialization.

PROFILE: Pingsha Dong

In the late 1990s, Dong was working at the Battelle Memorial Institute[1] as a welding engineer/senior research leader, with interest in predicting fatigue for welding joints. Metal fatigue is a primary cause of weld failure, and predicting those failures was an elusive goal of considerable research. Dong's key discovery/insight/aha! moment was to measure force *exerted on the joints* rather than to measure the stress they were undergoing. He developed a method to do so and validated its use for predicting metal fatigue. Discussions with colleagues at Battelle[2] encouraged him to think about his methodology as a valuable innovation, with applications in multiple markets that rely on welded materials, including aerospace, automotive, bridge construction, and other major industries.

Dong's invention was patented[3] and packaged into a product called Verity˚, which enables accurate prediction of weld fatigue regardless of welding components. He and his method won numerous awards, and Dong was named as a Time Magazine Math Innovator in 2005. The product Verity˚ was licensed to Safe Technology, which in turn introduced it to the market a year later as fe-safe˚. That product had considerable market success, which led Dassault Systèmes to buy Safe Technologies a few years later.

Throughout his career at Battelle, Dong actively published his work in scholarly journals. In 2009, he moved to academia, taking an endowed chair at the University of New Orleans. A few years later he moved to the University of Michigan, where he is an endowed professor and Director of the Welded Structures

Beyond Discovery. Jean E. Schelhorn and Joan M. Herbers, Oxford University Press. © Oxford University Press 2022. DOI: 10.1093/oso/9780197512715.003.0016

Laboratory. Dong is a prolific scholar, with 20 publications in 2020 alone, and directs a large laboratory. Most important for our purposes, he revolutionized the world of welding, thereby improving our lives as consumers and users of machinery and materials that rely on welded joints.

9

Is This for You?

I never said it would be easy; I only said it would be worth it.

—Mae West

Every researcher is enamored of their discoveries and rightly so. Whether an important discovery finds its way to market, though, requires more than personal passion; it requires a team of partners, strategy, and hard-headed financial decisions. You can (and must) be involved in some of those plans and decisions, and only you can say if that effort is worth it.

There are plenty of discouraging data. Most academic inventions are never licensed.[1] Small business and start-ups license far more academic inventions than corporations with deep pockets.[2] Patent applications from academic centers ultimately issue about two-thirds of the time, and it takes an average of three years.[3] Most commercialization offices operate at a loss.[4] In short, there are no guarantees of success.

Yet for some academics, the desire for societal good—meeting that compelling need in want of a solution—is enough for them to engage in the commercialization process. We hope this book has provided you with sufficient background to understand what that means and how you can influence the outcome.

You now know that commercialization takes many forms, with a common thread that inventions only leave research institutions via legally binding agreements. You also know that you do not need to start a company for your discoveries to reach markets. In this book, these twin insights encapsulate important

Beyond Discovery. Jean E. Schelhorn and Joan M. Herbers, Oxford University Press. © Oxford University Press 2022. DOI: 10.1093/oso/9780197512715.003.0017

messages: (1) commercialization includes business agreements with legally binding terms, which means that in most cases you must rely on others to support and propel the effort; and (2) finding the best path for your discovery requires the help and support of professionals beyond your domain. Understanding the resources available to you and cultivating a positive collaborative relationship with tech transfer are imperatives!

It is unlikely that your first try will hit; after all, how many experiments work immediately? A truism in this world is that an individual's second or third invention is much more likely to be patented/find a licensee: you learn how it is done by practicing. So do not be discouraged! Continue with your line of research because another discovery may become an invention that leads to a commercially relevant product or process that then becomes successful in the market. Serial inventors develop pattern-recognition skills, avoid inadvertent enabling disclosures, keep an eye on patent art, and know how they can contribute to marketing. If your first try goes nowhere, focus on what you have learned from that effort: as Henry Ford remarked, "Failure is simply the opportunity to begin again, this time more intelligently."

If you are a laboratory director (e.g., faculty member), this may not be for you—you have a demanding job—but it might be for your postdocs and grad students. Fostering the interest of protégés to engage in technology transfer in its many forms is perhaps even more important than engaging in it yourself. Junior scientists are often eager to learn about commercialization and can be very effective conduits for lab discoveries to reach markets. Furthermore, many a student starts a company after graduation. Allowing your students to explore options for technology translation while in your laboratory can have long-term payoffs.

Providing both context and guidelines for the translation of academic research results to market acceptance is the unmet need that motivated us to write this book. No book can answer every question, and so we have referred you to other volumes for deeper understanding. Our hope is that we have provided enough context that when a great insight hits you, or stunning proof of concept experiments are successful, you know how to get started. Please pass our book on!

So now you know the basics of how to use commercialization as a route to amplify the impact of your research. It isn't easy or fast, but it surely can be worth it. The topics presented here might change your mindset and your career trajectory, or perhaps they will help you encourage a lab member to move forward in unexpected ways. You have the potential to change our world.

Good luck!

PROFILE: Commercialization in the U.S. Department of Agriculture

In the United States, federal research laboratories are housed in most cabinet-level departments. Examples include the National Labs (Department of Energy), the National Institutes of Health (Health and Human Services), and the National Oceanic and Atmospheric Administration (Commerce). These units report annually to Congress concerning their technology transfer initiatives. Here we highlight research conducted in laboratories overseen by the United States Department of Agriculture (USDA), and how that research moves into the marketplace.

The USDA includes the Agricultural Research Service (ARS), National Forest Service, and Food Safety and Inspection Service, among other agencies, that employ thousands of scientists at more than 100 research facilities. Those scientists work on problems broadly related to agricultural production, and many are co-located on university campuses to facilitate scientific exchange. The ARS Mission statement states that it "delivers scientific solutions to national and global agricultural challenges." Examples of products on the market that have origins in USDA labs include lactose-free milk, organic pest-control agents, and many varieties of seedless grapes. To achieve its mission, the ARS actively solicits input from stakeholders concerning areas where research is needed. Stakeholder groups include academic scientists, commodities groups (e.g., almond-growers, pig breeders), other federal agencies, and businesses.

This focus epitomizes "pull commercialization" whereby clear, large, validated unmet market needs drive the research agenda. Accordingly, tech transfer is integrated with that research agenda,

Beyond Discovery. Jean E. Schelhorn and Joan M. Herbers, Oxford University Press. © Oxford University Press 2022. DOI: 10.1093/oso/9780197512715.003.0018

which ensures that USDA research translates into improved agricultural products and practices.[1]

Mojdeh Bahar is the Assistant Administrator for the ARS Office of Technology Transfer (OTT). Bahar is herself a patent attorney, with an extensive background in federal laboratories, and she is passionate about her mission to bring USDA research to market. Her office has specific responsibilities much like those in academia: they negotiate licenses with external entities, they handle CRADAs, MTAs and DTAs, and they develop and file patent applications. In 2020, her office filed 76 patent applications, and 50 patents were issued; they had 565 active licenses and 430 research collaborations that involve IP provisions, and they also processed hundreds of MTAs. In addition, they participated in preparing proposals for SBIR and STTR grants led by small businesses collaborating with ARS scientists.

Just as academic institutions are challenged to incorporate tech transfer into their cultures, the USDA Office of Technology Transfer has worked hard to become successful partners and teammates with ARS scientists. They proactively provide well-attended training such as on-site workshops, online training modules, and regular communications with both scientists and external stakeholders. They have initiated an internal I-Corps program, and they offer seed grants from an Innovation Fund. Recognition programs highlight successes, and receipt of an award is considered prestigious within the agency.

Interest in tech transfer is steadily growing as ARS scientists come to understand how commercialization can amplify the impact of their work. We strongly encourage academic institutions to learn from federal research agencies and to consider applying those lessons to build commercialization into their own culture.

Epilogue: Messages to Administrators and Commercialization Staff

We have primarily written for academic researchers, and we now offer some thoughts to those with whom they work.

To Administrators

As Vice Presidents, Provosts, Deans, and Department Chairs, you lead discussions to set policies that affect the way researchers think and behave. Throughout our book we have referenced policies concerning intellectual property, conflicts of interest, revenue-sharing, and the like. These policies are important to your institution's agenda of translating research to the society at large, to be sure. Now we encourage you to examine all your policies to assess whether in fact they encourage researchers to *engage* in that agenda and the commercialization office staff to effectively encourage and *manage* that agenda.

No policy can make a dent in any researcher's behavior or attitude unless it aligns with the rewards system. Tenure and promotion standards are the clearest description of any institution's academic values.[1] National bodies have called for these standards to include metrics related to commercialization, such as invention reports, issued patents, and licenses,[2] and many universities are following suit. Even so, standards related to traditional academic metrics such as publications, teaching, and service still predominate in decisions

Beyond Discovery. Jean E. Schelhorn and Joan M. Herbers, Oxford University Press. © Oxford University Press 2022. DOI: 10.1093/oso/9780197512715.003.0019

concerning promotion and tenure. If units do not include commercialization metrics in their standards,[3] then such activities are likely to fly below a faculty member's radar.[4] Furthermore, as we discussed in Chapter 8, omission of such metrics disproportionately discourages women and (non-Asian) minorities from considering tech transfer.

We also strongly suggest that you examine whether your science and engineering graduate programs are providing sufficient information and encouragement to students (and postdocs) concerning commercialization. Many of these trainees are eager to learn about careers outside academia,[5] and universities that target student involvement have more robust tech transfer enterprises.[6] Indeed, start-up companies are more often founded by former students and postdocs than by faculty and research staff,[7] and former students who work in industry are important contacts for your institution's commercialization agenda. Because most graduate education and virtually all of postdoctoral training is decentralized in the STEM disciplines, you must engage faculty PIs in discussions about how to broaden their training and mentoring programs.

We also suggest that you highlight for researchers the problem of unintended public disclosure. Certainly, training and then reminding them about public disclosure are both important, but rarely adequate to prevent problems. A best practice in some institutions is to ask the tech transfer office (or other administrator with sufficient background) to screen for potential IP in manuscripts, posters, grant proposals, and the like *prior to submission or during the ensuing confidential period*. Your office may not have the bandwidth or commercial perspective to conduct rapid turnaround screens, and you can expect pushback from researchers. However, once such practices are embedded within the institutional culture, the likelihood of unintended public disclosure is substantially diminished.

We also encourage you to seek information on and specifically highlight the *impact* of research done in your institution.[8] As we described in Chapter 1, research is prompted by both investigator curiosity and a desire to solve big Problems. Devising metrics related to impact itself can also further the commercialization agenda.

Exemplars exist within our federal lab system (see the profile of the USDA Office of Technology Transfer), where every researcher is asked to describe the ways in which the research has moved into product/service development. While not every discipline, research area, or invention can be translated to the marketplace, yet all should be able to demonstrate impact on student training, knowledge creation, and understanding. Indeed, students are the most effective conduit for taking institutional expertise into the world at large.

If your institution has not yet done so, we also encourage you to examine policies concerning the use of research space. Many private universities allow faculty to house start-up companies in their laboratories, and even some public universities, bound by local laws, are now finding ways to co-locate businesses.[9] Others are able to offer space in privately funded research parks or incubators in order to keep start-up companies close to founders. For faculty considering starting a company, having proximity to equipment and minds in the research lab itself can be a deciding factor.

Administrators pay attention to rankings. Academic institutions that lead the rankings for technology transfer[10] are characterized foremost by (1) superb research enterprises; (2) highly effective commercialization offices that move inventions out the door via robust marketing; and (3) a local ecosystem that pulls inventions out via strong interactions with the institution. If you advise or supervise the tech transfer office at your institution, we suggest that you examine how the top-ranked ones are structured, how they work, how they became top-ranked, and how they adapt as the markets for their products shift over time. For example, in Chapter 6 we described Stanford's decision to eliminate a requirement for certain kinds of MTA-out agreements in 2010. Many institutions followed suit, yet yours may still be spending precious time cutting MTA-out agreements, some of which may not be necessary. You can ask your external peers about best practices and consider whether your institution can shift its practices and policies accordingly. When examining how peers structure their commercialization enterprises, keep in mind exemplars in quasi-academic institutions.[11]

Finally, we suggest that you expand the way you evaluate your professional staff in the commercialization office. Metrics like patent applications and invention disclosures primarily reflect internal processing and fail to capture what really matters: how often and how quickly those inventions are licensed. Remember that the definition of technology transfer is technology moving out of your institution: inventions cannot have meaningful impact unless they are licensed to third parties.

License agreements can be cut years (yes, years) after an invention report, which puts a premium on active marketing to shorten that time lag.[12] Licensing is necessary but not sufficient for successful commercialization, of course; the licensee must work hard to actually move the licensed invention to market and to become profitable. Even so, keeping the focus on license deals places emphasis on the end game—and also can generate revenue for your institution.

To the Tech Transfer/Commercialization Office

Your office is a crucial service hub. You interface with inventors, administrators, patent attorneys, industry representatives, investors, and government representatives. Developing relationships with all of them is part of your mission, and here we focus on the partnership that you and the inventor must develop. If you work in academia, keep in mind that commercialization activity is not a *requirement* but rather an *option* for faculty and student researchers.[13] Their main focus is on the research itself, and they know that in most institutions grants bring in more money to the university than your office does. In short, inventors approach you out of interest and potential impact, and you must work to keep that interest alive: yours is a service organization.

Regular and consistent communication with the inventor and their departments and deans is essential. The inventor knows more about the technology than anyone else, and your job is to learn enough of the technical details to guide and in some cases drive the path toward the market. Your communications with the inventor should be as free as possible of jargon and legalese.[14] You can further the partnership via regular updates on your efforts and also by asking for progress updates on their technology. Communications should be copied to those within the higher levels of the inventor's circle, which serves not only to highlight their work but also to embed commercialization within your institution's culture.

Be the partner you would like them to be: go to *their* office, then stay for a bit, and walk around to learn about other research programs down the hall. Simply being there sometimes provokes fruitful discussions with students, administrators, postdocs, and lab leaders. It also reinforces the key message that your job is to serve the researcher and help their work matter in a larger context.

We also encourage you to ask permission to screen proposals/manuscripts/publications/slide decks, and other materials. Such reviews are critical to avoid public disclosure of potential inventions, of course, and in this way you might avert last-minute fire drills. Furthermore, reviewing those materials can help you understand the breadth of what the lab is working on and possibly give you ideas about new paths for marketing their inventions. You are more likely to receive such permission to review if you have cultivated positive relationships and commit to turn the materials around quickly.

Once a provisional patent application or a utility patent application is filed, you know the timeline for the next steps within your office. Make sure you remind the inventor of important dates and give them enough time to respond; in turn, request that they turn materials around to you with sufficient time. Academic researchers understand deadlines, to be sure, but their own always take precedence!

Finally, it is your job to market the invention to potential licensees; the technology goes nowhere without a license. We strongly encourage you to enlist the inventor as a willing partner. With clear and consistent communication established, the inventor will surely reach out to you with any potential licensees they know, learn of, and meet. You can market an invention only to the extent that you understand it and have thought about potential market plays with the inventor and colleagues. Broaden that perspective by periodically reviewing your portfolio with office-mates.[15] In our experience, success in signing a license deal is a function of the effort you put into marketing the technology.[16]

Once you have cut a license deal (Congratulations!), we offer two more suggestions. First, let the inventor be one of the first to know of the deal! Astoundingly, some academics are not among the first to learn, or they learn very late, that their discovery has been licensed. Second, when you do alert the inventor of a successful license deal, make sure they understand any confidentiality requirements that are part of the deal. Then it is time to celebrate!

We hope the information in Chapter 8 gave you pause and caused you to think about your experiences with women and inventors of color. Understanding that not all inventors think alike or have the same motivations can help you serve everyone better. Unconscious bias is pervasive in our society, and we encourage you to learn about your own biases (we all have them) at implicit.harvard.edu, where you will also find a wealth of resources on this important topic. Every inventor should have the same opportunities to change the world, and your gatekeeper role is critical for providing equal access.

Sometimes you must give an inventor disappointing news. Perhaps your office has decided not to pursue a patent, or patent prosecution is not going well. You may have been unable to identify a licensee for the technology within a reasonable time period, or an optionee may decide not to exercise the option. Regardless of why efforts stall, you should have an in-depth conversation with the inventor and describe their alternatives, in near-real time. Furthermore, encourage them to come back with the next invention and stay in touch—most often the second, third, or fourth invention is more successful.

The above considerations highlight our major point of view: you may currently be operating in push mode with researchers. Once they approach you, then you get to work. However, that passive approach allows you to tap into only a fraction of your institution's creativity. Consider a pull model instead: find out what researchers do, discuss with them the nature of their discoveries, reframe in the language of invention, and then work with them to initiate and complete formal processes. Such an approach can spark a researcher's interest in translation and is highly contagious to their colleagues.

In our book we have stressed that successful commercialization is a team sport. Some inventors choose to stay on the bench and others want more active roles. Some departments and colleges are rooting in the stands and others are barely aware that your office exists. To paraphrase a common American expression,[17] there is no I in technology transfer. You play a central role in setting the commercialization agenda, and keeping the needs of academic researchers in mind will help you (and your institution) serve them well.

In closing, we wish you every success on this incredible quest. Changing the world starts in the researcher's lab, and your role is to help propel a discovery into the hands of an entity that can take it to market for lasting impact. How cool is that?

Acronyms

AAAS	American Association for the Advancement of Science
AAU	American Association of Universities
AAUP	American Association of University Professors
APLU	Association of Public and Land-grant Universities
ARS	Agricultural Research Service (part of the USDA)
AUTM	Association of University Technology Managers
BARDA	Biomedical Advanced Research and Development Authority
C-Suite	Upper leadership, with "Chief" in their titles such as CEO, CSO
CDA	Confidential Disclosure Agreement
CEO	Chief Executive Officer
COVID-19	The disease caused by SARS-CoV-2
CRADA	Cooperative Research and Development Agreement
CSO	Chief Scientific Officer
DNA	Deoxyribonucleic acid
DOD	Department of Defense
DOE	Department of Energy
DTA	Data Transfer Agreement
EC	Evaluation Criteria
FDA	Food and Drug Administration
FRE	Fundamental Research Exclusion
GUIRR	Government – University – Industry Research Roundtable
I-CORPS	Innovation Corps
IIA	Inter-institutional Agreement
IP	Intellectual Property
IPDR	Intellectual Property Disclosure Report
IPO	Initial Public Offering
IR	Invention Report
IRS	Internal Revenue Service
LES	Licensing Executive Society
mRNA	messenger RNA (ribonucleic acid)
MTA	Material Transfer Agreement
NASA	National Aeronautics and Space Administration
NASEM	National Academies of Science, Engineering, and Mathematics
NDA	Nondisclosure Agreement

NGO	Nongovernmental organization
NIH	National Institutes of Health
NSF	National Science Foundation
PCT	Patent Cooperation Treaty
PI	Principal Investigator
RFP	Request for Proposals
SARS-CoV-2	the virus that causes COVID-19
SBA	Small Business Administration
SBIR	Small Business Innovation Research
STEM	Science, Technology, Engineering, and Mathematics
STTR	Small Business Technology Transfer
TRL	Technology Readiness Level
TTO	Technology Transfer Office/Officer
UBMTA	Unified Biological Material Transfer Agreement
USDA	United States Department of Agriculture
USPTO	United States Patent and Trademark Office
VC	Venture Capital/Capitalist
VP	Value Proposition
WARF	Wisconsin Alumni Research Foundation
WIPO	World Intellectual Property Organization

Notes

Introduction

1. See Kirchberger and Pohl (2016) for a review.
2. Gruber and Johnson (2019).
3. See the recent report from the National Academies (NASEM, 2019).
4. www.compete.org. In fact, many states have set up such commissions as well.
5. Technology transfer refers both to offices within institutions and to the processes that professional staff use to move research discoveries out of the institution and into the private sector.
6. Hockaday (2020) has written a complementary volume explaining how technology transfer works from an administrator's view.
7. Important variables in the United States include private versus public universities; the balance among research, teaching, and service; and the extent of decentralization within institutions.

Chapter 1

1. In Chapters 4 and 6 you will learn about "when."
2. And, of course, our students who move into the workforce represent perhaps our most effective means of disseminating research results.
3. Which could be you!
4. Roach and Sauermann (2010); Campbell and O'Meara (2014).
5. Development of careers is highly individualized. For many, teaching is a primary motivator, especially in 2- and 4-year colleges. For others, research is a primary motivator, such as in larger universities with a strong research mission. We focus on this latter group and stress that motivation to do research does not imply that other responsibilities are shirked.
6. We write this volume during the COVID-19 pandemic, when so many have pivoted to urgent needs for equipment retrofitting, vaccine development, sterilization methods, and so on. A shared sense of responsibility has caused legions of researchers to examine how their expertise can contribute to fighting the novel coronavirus, and new private–public partnerships have been forged toward that end as well. Their responses to the pandemic emergency vividly illustrate that researchers want to help solve big Problems.

7. Metrics for commercialization are starting to appear in the rewards system, but that movement is slow and localized, despite the position papers published by the National Academies of Science, Engineering, and Medicine (NASEM 2020b) and the Association of Public and Land-Grant Universities (APLU 2015).

8. Indeed, research "impact" is usually measured by citation indices and journal impact factors, which are unconnected with societal impact.

9. In multiple contexts beyond commercialization! For example, scientists rarely contact the media; they wait for reporters to call them.

10. There is a third mindset that is particularly challenging: many researchers simply have an "ick" reaction to the possibility of commercial plays for their work. A common response to our presentations is, "If I had wanted to go into business, I would have." We hope to change a few of those mindsets.

11. Often referred to as market-facing.

12. This ploy is prevalent in the health sciences, perhaps the most explicitly hierarchical of all academic disciplines. Identification as a "thought leader" is highly valued, especially by physicians.

13. Throughout this volume, we use the term *partnership* in its generic sense, unless explicitly stated otherwise.

14. Wisnioski and Vinsel (2019).

15. One of our colleagues compared engaging in commercialization to crossing the Grand Canyon.

16. Another apparent disincentive we have heard about is the fear that commercialization will take valuable time away from traditional research. Yet the available data show that there is no such negative effect (Buenstorf 2009).

17. Howe et al. (2014).

18. Indeed, Hockaday (2020) maintains this is the raison d'etre for technology transfer: the returns to society as a whole are more important than the returns to the university.

19. See the Epilogue for specific recommendations for administrators.

20. Indeed, U.S. federal laboratories are required to have offices of technology transfer, per the 1980 Stevenson-Wydler Technology Act. See our Profile on the U.S. Department of Agriculture's programs.

21. Link and Scott (2019) argue that federal labs are uniquely positioned to develop technologies and then transfer them to the private sector.

22. https://www.federallabs.org

23. Others are supported on fellowships, teaching assistantships, and the like.

24. See the Biomedical Research Workforce Working Group report (2012).

25. Stenard and Sauermann (2016) describe dissatisfaction as a major motivator for entrepreneurs from many employment sectors to start businesses. The highly respected *Chronicle of Higher Education* collects personal accounts from academics who have left higher education in its "Quit Lit" section. Cassuto and

Weinbuch (2021) analyze this problem and call for an entirely new approach to graduate programs.

26. Mason et al. (2013).

27. Cassuto and Weinbuch (2021). An active blogosphere provides tips on how to become an entrepreneur, on sites hosted by the American Association for the Advancement of Science, the National Postdoctoral Association, and numerous groups abroad.

28. We explore the common mistakes that limit protection of intellectual property in Chapter 6.

29. Numerous other career paths exist for which graduate students should be prepared as well (Cassuto and Weinbuch 2021).

30. Indeed, fields that attract industry funding, especially in engineering, already have implemented such training.

31. Hayter et al. (2016); Beyhan and Findik (2018).

32. New programs explicitly link science and engineering graduates with entrepreneurship training. For example, the University of Memphis Patents2Products postdoctoral fellowships provide support for new PhDs to investigate commercial possibilities for their research.

33. Indeed, we have noticed that young faculty are considerably more interested in translating their work to the marketplace.

PROFILE: Patrick Brown

1. May 2020 podcast, available at https://www.npr.org/podcasts/510313/how-i-built-this

2. We have tried the product and can personally attest to its high quality. No more tofu burgers for us.

3. Searches conducted in February 2021 on USPTO.gov; patents.google.com; and https://impossiblefoods.com

Chapter 2

1. For a stunning representation of the landscape for SARS-Cov-2 vaccine development, see https://www.nature.com/articles/s41587-021-00912-9/figures/1. This figure shows a network of entities and their relationships. Companies, universities, and funding agencies are all involved in vaccine development against this viral scourge. Patent applications, license deals, legal challenges, and other details illustrate the complexity emerging in product development/production for critical vaccine candidates.

2. And we offer a bare minimum of terms! We have collected these in the Glossary.

3. You may also hear about intellectual capital, which encompasses people, structures/physical assets, and relationships with other parties.

4. There is also know-what (facts) and know-why (understanding).

5. In the United States, this is governed by IRS Code Title 26, subchapter F, section 501.

6. We define all the kinds of institutionally funded research in Chapter 5.

7. Novelty is one of three criteria required for patenting, as we describe in Chapter 4.

8. Small institutions may not have an infrastructure to support technology transfer. We offer suggestions on navigating this situation in Chapter 6.

9. For example, the Pacific Northwest Transportation Consortium (depts.washington.edu/pactrans) serves all transportation-related researchers in the Northwest region.

10. We provide more detail on all of these roles in subsequent chapters.

11. We use this language instead of "contract" or other wording. With this term, we wish to convey that commercialization requires a legal agreement beyond a memorandum of understanding or other nonbinding document. All the agreements we discuss in this chapter have legal dimensions, and we use "agreement" to denote a legally binding agreement.

12. A nonexclusive grant of rights is common for copyright materials, in licenses conferred via the Material Transfer Agreement (MTA), and others.

13. In most MTAs, the grant of rights is restricted to the recipient institution and the material use is under the direction of the recipient PI.

14. The word *term* has a technical meaning for a license/option denoting time. It also may be used in the agreement itself in other contexts. Note that academics often use "term" to mean "semester," so don't get confused!

15. We cover these in detail in Chapter 4.

16. Much more on MTAs, Data Transfer Agreements (DTAs), and confidential disclosure agreements (CDAs) awaits you in Chapter 6.

17. An additional category that conveys a grant of rights through an option agreement is an industry-sponsored research agreement, discussed in Chapter 5. Other circumstances may require specialized agreements.

18. A business plan can be a condition of the next logical step, a license agreement.

19. A lot is implied in this sentence! We cover the most important topics in Chapter 4.

20. Another mandatory move to licensing occurs if the optionee secures federal grant funding (Small Business Innovation Research (SBIR), Small Business Technology Transfer STTR)) as we describe in Chapter 7.

21. However, selling products or services is not permitted under an option agreement.

22. The optionee at its own discretion can incur considerable additional costs outside the license agreement, such as market assessment services, patent attorney fees for various studies, and possible research activities.

23. There may be such a template on your institution's website. Examples can be found at

https://www.anl.gov/sites/www/files/2019-09/Express%20Option%20Agreement_20190914.pdf

https://www.innovation.pitt.edu/wp-content/uploads/2018/05/PCO-Start-Up-Option-Template-2018.pdf

https://www.shawnee.edu/sites/default/files/documents/Option%20Agreement%20Template.pdf

24. This is a legal term with meaning quite distinct from what faculty often think of concerning grant expenditures. An encumbrance/encumberment is a grant of rights already given to another party.

25. Examples of license agreement templates follow, with the final link showing a range of agreement templates.

http://innovation.ucsd.edu/wp-content/uploads/2016/08/OpenFlowInventionLicenseJuly_2016.pdf

http://www.ott.emory.edu/documents/agree_templates/emory_exclusive_agree_template.pdf

https://otd.harvard.edu/industry-investors/sample-agreements/licensing

26. Equity is a stake in the company, meaning partial ownership.

27. Discretionary accounts are highly prized in academia!

28. We write this book during the SARS-CoV-2 pandemic, which has placed a priority on quick scale-up of promising technologies. In this environment, we have seen many early-stage licensees of technology (especially in the vaccine space) sublicensing or selling their positions to larger companies that can deliver product in scale to market customers. See our Profile on Katalin Karikó for a timely example.

29. Evergreen agreements have no grant of right to assets that have an associated expiration date. Examples might include nonpatented items or data. They might also be referred to as a perpetual license. These terms are just names for different flavors of agreements: they are all license agreements.

30. And that is a very good thing. Your time is better spent doing what you do best: research, teaching, and service.

31. White and Burg (2019).

32. These terms have nuances of meaning that we can mostly ignore for academic institutions. Hereafter we use "start-up," and we explore them fully in Chapter 7.

33. AUTM (2018).

34. With one gigantic exception: if you decide to start a company! See Chapter 7 for how that works.

Chapter 3

1. https://www.pitt.edu/chancellor/commercialization
2. Johnson (2017) explores this cultural divide in great depth.
3. See also Khor (2014), who provides insights tailored to biomedical research.
4. http://parisinnovationreview.com/articles-en/three-ways-to-drive-innovation
5. This word was coined by the Alcoa Corporation for its business and has been extensively used by the Disney Corporation.
6. In industry, teams from marketing (deep market and channel understanding) and R&D (technical and manufacturing understanding) collaborate to envision new products/processes and imagine/project how they might play in a variety of markets. If a potentially profitable market concept emerges, they can target the innovation for that market.
7. See Roberts (1989) for many fun stories.
8. Much ink has been spilled on the topic of basic versus applied research, which we consider a dubious and distracting dichotomy.
9. There is an interesting tension between applied research and commercialization, especially in publicly funded institutions. Many academic researchers feel that their work should be freely given away, especially if it was funded by taxpayer dollars. Industry is well aware of this attitude.
10. https://www.covidinnovations.com/
11. folding@home.org
12. opencovidpledge.org
13. https://otl.stanford.edu/COVID-19-technology-access-framework
14. https://www.uspto.gov/coronavirus
15. Singer (2014).
16. Few academics realize that most tech transfer offices operate at a net loss (Wisnioski and Vinsel 2019).
17. There is an analog with your Sponsored Programs Office, where the division of responsibilities between you and that office is clear. Yet that office does not essentially judge your grant proposals, nor does it contract with external experts to assess them. The work done by the commercialization office is considerably more intricate and opaque to you; it must make decisions concerning your invention, and you may need to provide additional information before that can happen. Cultivating a strong partnership over years characterizes the engaged academic inventor.
18. And they are likely enamored of theirs as well.
19. Students funded on grants/contracts are subject to institutional IP policy. However, students who, say, start software companies in their dorms are not.
20. Stenard and Sauermann (2016).

21. Cassuto and Weisbuch (2021).
22. This frustrates tech transfer staff to no end. One officer remarked that it can take weeks and repeated phone calls just to get a professor to sign and return a form.
23. We illustrate with the experience of JMH. She settled on solving the fundamental problem of polygyny in ant nests (e.g., having more than one laying queen) in the summer of 1980; it took 15 years to amass all the lines of evidence to explain why ant queens of some species cohabit cooperatively. The answer, to quote Lucy Van Pelt from the *Peanuts* comic strip, is real estate. If you want to know more, drop us a line.
24. Diamandis and Bouras (2018) have an interesting take on this phenomenon in science. Several commentators have described how physician hubris interferes with the practice of good medicine (Bergman 1986).
25. Cf. Fanelli (2010).
26. Unless they themselves become the licensee in the context of a start-up company; we cover these issues in Chapter 7.
27. We cover public disclosure at length in Chapter 6. Academics are masters at asking forgiveness rather than permission, but not every action can be forgiven.
28. Mistakes are commonplace in research as in every human endeavor. However, there is no room for poor experimental design or data fudging in any path toward commercialization.
29. Patent attorneys must present background education in science or engineering.
30. Hardré and Kollmann (2012).
31. Sanberg et al. (2014); Genschaft et al. (2016). See also position papers from the Association of Public and Land-grant Universities (APLU, 2015) and the National Academies of Sciences, Engineering, and Medicine (NASEM, 2020b).
32. Support of commercialization from the department chair (Greven et al. 2020) and peers (Perkmann et al. 2021) are key to engaging faculty and shifting local culture.

PROFILE: Katalin Karikó

1. The entire world owes Karikó a debt of gratitude for her persistence in this pioneering work.
2. As of September 2021, there are over 1800 clinical trials based on mRNA technology (clinicaltrials.gov).
3. The Pfizer-BioNTech COVID-19 vaccine was fully approved for use in the United States in August 2021, to be marketed as Comirnaty®.

Chapter 4

1. We restrict our coverage to systems used in the United States, with occasional reference to international bodies.
2. We have known many scientists and engineers who have shifted careers to move into patent law, and perhaps this will strike a chord with you! Sources for detailed information in patent law include https://www.uspto.gov/learning-and-resources/patent-and-trademark-practitioners/becoming-patent-practitioner.
3. https://www.copyright.gov provides details of U.S. copyright law and allows creators to register their works. It also describes treaties that provide international copyright protection for residents of signatory countries.
4. Academic institutions own many trademarks and registered trademarks, of course (think t-shirts featuring sports mascots). In rare cases, these are relevant to outputs of research, and we ignore them until Chapter 7.
5. https://www.justia.com/intellectual-property/trademarks/trade-dress. Trade dress refers to the "look and feel" of a product. One can often tell what a product is by its colors, shape of packaging, size, and so on: its trade dress.
6. Trade secrets refer to a spectrum of technical and business information that gives competitive advantage. Protection for trade secrets is afforded by maintaining the trade secret information confidential. If secrecy is not maintained or others discover the same information, protection is lost. Trade secrets cannot be held on any information gained or derived from federal funding, and they are more common in industry than academia. Patents have a finite life, but trade secrets can be held for as long as the information remains confidential. A commonly discussed trade secret is the formula for Coca-Cola.
7. Article I, Section 8, Clause 8, of the United States Constitution grants Congress the enumerated power "To promote the progress of science and useful arts, by securing for limited times to authors and inventors the exclusive right to their respective writings and discoveries."
8. Academic institutions typically cannot do this directly but can provide a grant of rights to the patent to an external party for commercialization purposes (Chapter 2).
9. Refer to the policies in your institution for details.
10. See Chapter 5 for a description of how IP rights flow from various funding sources.
11. This is an entire topic in itself. A patent can be "abandoned" if the assignee decides not to pay maintenance fees, or it can be invalidated through official challenges in court.
12. In an extreme case, the assignee can continue prosecution of a case with multiple inventions through divisional filings. Typically, only one invention can be reflected in each issued patent.

13. A patent agent is recognized by the U.S. Patent and Trademark Office (USPTO) after passing an exam. A patent attorney is a patent agent who also has a law degree. All patent attorneys are patent agents but not the reverse.

14. An issued patent does not give the inventor a monopoly but does provide commercially valuable rights.

15. United States Code, Section 271.

16. The development time for a new drug is notoriously long and usually consumes a large percentage of the patent life.

17. In the United States the protection provided to processes by utility patents can include business methods (see *Bilski v Kappos*, 130 S. Ct. 3218 [2010]) and software (see *Alice Corp. v. CLS Bank International*, 573 US 208 [2014]).

18. Design patents have a life of 15 years from the grant date if the design patent application was filed on or after May 13, 2015.

19. The grant for a plant patent, which lasts 20 years from the date of filing the application, protects the patent owner's right to exclude others from asexually reproducing the plant, and from using, offering for sale, or selling the plant so reproduced, or any of its parts, throughout the United States, or from importing the plant so reproduced, or any part thereof, into the United States.

20. Data from AUTM (2018) reports that utility patents represent 80% and plant patents 20% of filings from academic institutions.

21. Individual countries have additional regulations for such formulations. In the United States, generic drugs must be approved for safety and efficacy by the Federal Drug Administration.

22. 35 US Code Section 101.

23. 35 US Code Section 171; these are virtually nonexistent in academic institutions.

24. 35 US Code Section 161.

25. By law, inventors own their inventions. If they move forward as the applicant for a patent and the patent issues, they own the patent. In academia and in most companies, the employees assign their rights in inventions to their employer (now the assignee and the owner). In academia, the assignee is usually the institution, but in some sponsored research agreements, the sponsor may be the assignee. See Chapter 5 where we describe requirements for title election steps for invention derived from federally supported research. Academic inventors and corporate inventors rarely own the right to inventions made created in the context of their employment.

26. Some academics want a patent for its own sake; these "vanity patents" are a poor use of the TTO's resources.

27. Not all patent filings reach allowed claims.

28. An application is sometimes called a filing, a case, and even a matter.

29. 35 US Code Sections 2, 3, 131, and 132.

30. Especially if there is a severe time crunch; we cover that topic in Chapter 6 and offer advice for avoiding it.
31. Such reviews help inform the decision whether or not a patent might issue if the application is filed and what might be the scope of claims issuance.
32. The search report is issued by the patent office to which the case is submitted. The USPTO generates a search report for U.S.-filed applications; other countries generate a search report for applications filed in their national patent offices, and so on. There is a provision for international filing that we cover later in this chapter on the Patent Cooperation Treaty (PCT), administered by the World Intellectual Property Organization (WIPO). PCT search reports are publicly available, but individual country search reports may not be.
33. You are allowed to fix typos and obvious errors in the specification.
34. If all claims are allowed immediately, that may indicate that the claims in the application were not broad enough; the analogy is that if you sell your house on day one at a higher price than the listing, you probably set the asking price too low!
35. Beyond the scope of this book are additional strategy steps that can be used after allowance of claims and prior to payment of issue fees.
36. See, for example, *Endo Pharma v. Teva* (2019), which on appeal found that a treatment for pain in renal patients that caused increased bio availability of a naturally occurring compound could be patented as a therapy. See also *UC v. Broad Institute* (2018), which affirmed that Broad's patent on CRISPR technology was sufficiently different from that developed in the University of California to satisfy the nonobviousness criterion.
37. See Chapter 6 where we categorize public disclosures as BIG MISTAKE #1.
38. Some concepts can be filed as an intellectual reduction to practice. In such a case, all the elements (pieces and parts) of the concept are fully known, and it meets the criteria for patentability.
39. https://www.wipo.int/pct/en/pct_contracting_states.html. That leaves 42 countries that are not signatories to the PCT.
40. The PCT provisions never override those of participating countries.
41. See https://www.wipo.int/pct/en/texts/time_limits.html
42. Known as freedom to operate.
43. This simplest form of infringement is direct infringement. There are also actions by unlicensed parties that can constitute "contributory infringement" and "inducing infringement."
44. Patent enforcement consists of actions taken by the licensee/assignee to assert their patent rights to exclude others from practicing the claimed invention.
45. All forms of IP should be enforced, including copyright and trademarks.
46. A particularly horrifying example is unprotected storage of data, manuscripts, and other products on unsecured public sites. This constitutes disclosure. Imagine the mess when it is discovered after a patent has been licensed.

47. Both naming noninventors and omitting real inventors from patent applications are reasons for invalidation. See our Profile on Ashim Mitra.
48. "Conception is the formation in the mind of the inventor of a definite and permanent idea of the complete and operative invention, as it is hereafter to be applied in practice." *Hybritech, Inc. v. Monoclonal Antibodies, Inc.,* 802 F.2d 1367, 1376 (Fed. Cir. 1986).
49. Academic centers typically qualify for small entity fees, which are usually half the amount charged to large entities for filing and other prosecution costs as set forth on the USPTO schedules. Start-up companies may in some cases qualify for micro-entity fees.
50. See the fee schedule at https://www.uspto.gov/sites/default/files/documents/USPTO%20fee%20schedule_current.pdf
51. A typical international filing strategy might include five to six countries, perhaps $250,000 in costs over the patent's term.
52. The maintenance fee schedule for the United States is at https://www.uspto.gov/learning-and-resources/fees-and-payment/uspto-fee-schedule#Patent%20Maintenance%20Fee
53. Key (2017) thinks that estimate is generous.
54. Recall that an issued patent allows the assignee and its licensee to exclude others in commerce from practicing the claims that are allowed within an issued patent. The true value of a patent is in claims use for commerce.
55. And we are intensely grateful for the help of our attorney friends.
56. The most comprehensive reference in this field is Chisum (1997). This 17-volume set (each volume weighs more than 5 pounds) is updated five times every year.

PROFILE: Ashim Mitra

1. News reports on this story:
   https://www.kcur.org/education/2019-02-26/umkc-says-pharmacy-professor-stole-students-research-and-sold-it-for-1-5-million
   University reaches $360,000 settlement with professor who said his boss used students as servants | UMKC Roo News
   UMKC settles lawsuit with professor accused of stealing research, receives $6.45M | UMKC Roo News

Chapter 5

1. Singer (2014).
2. Cleary et al. (2018).

3. Except for education materials and other products covered by copyright. Academic institutions have the convention of automatically assigning copyright IP to faculty authors; see Chapter 4.

4. In addition to institutional policy, government funders typically require assignment to the institution of any assets developed with that funding.

5. Do not confuse start-up funds with start-up companies! In academic institutions, new faculty hires are provided start-up funds so that they can develop research programs quickly. In some disciplines, hiring start-up costs can exceed $1M for a beginning faculty member and $10M for a star being hired at the Professor level. Amounts at smaller institutions are considerably lower.

6. To add to the confusion: some gifts are actually called grants by the donor. The distinction between a gift and a sponsored agreement can cause discord between faculty members and their institutions. For example, some foundations provide both gifts and sponsored research agreements to academic institutions; faculty strongly prefer to receive such support as gifts because little or no overhead is charged. Careful negotiation with the entity is needed to reveal whether the funds constitute a gift or a sponsored agreement.

7. A study of Italian patenting showed that institutional funds led to more original patents (Guerzoni et al. 2014).

8. See https://tomkat.stanford.edu/innovation-transfer and https://www.cit.org/crcf.html for two examples.

9. For example, the NIH Clinical and Translational Awards Program gives awards to academic institutions, with an explicit emphasis on translational research; the parent grant can provide small incentive grants to individual investigators.

10. There are, of course, other kinds of grants in universities, such as for student aid.

11. Unless, of course, there is misconduct or malfeasance.

12. Commodities/special interest groups such as almond growers or animal health charities actively fund targeted research in universities.

13. Of course, there are exceptions. Some entities do give grants directly to individuals, and often the institution is not even informed. Examples include many competitive fellowships (e.g., Guggenheim, Fulbright) as well as small grants from some nonprofits.

14. Indeed, one of us was co-PI on a federal grant proposal that was approved by program officers but given an "administrative decline" because certain nonnegotiable conditions could not be met that involved the business practices of the submitting organization.

15. Stevens (2004) gives a fascinating account of how this bill came to be enacted and what a close call it was.

16. This legal term covers all entities receiving federal grants.

17. Reduction to practice is the series of steps taken that move an idea past conception. Typically, this means that you have actually shown that the idea/conception works.

18. Details for the various steps required and the timeline for each are available at https://public.era.nih.gov/iedison/public/timeline.jsp.

19. Prior to passage of the Bayh-Dole Act, the federal government held exclusive ownership of any discovery made from their grants.

20. This act has numerous other conditions, including prohibition of trade secrets and a requirement to manufacture substantially in the United States.

21. If we consider all federal agency grant funds since 1980, this means that trillions of dollars have been leveraged.

22. See Audretsch and Link (2017).

23. The Bayh-Dole Act also spurred other countries to institute new policies for commercializing academic research (Gores and Link 2021).

24. An intriguing exception is state-funded research in California on human stem cells, which was outlawed by the U.S. government in 2001. See Mireles (2006) for an overview.

25. See https://blog.ecivis.com/bid/118832/pass-through-grants-what-they-re-all-about.

26. Michelson (2020); https://sciencephilanthropyalliance.org.

27. Read the funding agreement and understand your obligations! The institution may be held in breach of contract if these requirements are not met. Indeed, we know of several instances when a nonprofit sponsor refused to make final payments.

28. Often the company will require a confidential disclosure agreement (CDA) to proceed with detailed discussions (see also Chapter 6).

29. Don't forget: institutional indirect costs will be included!

30. This consideration takes us to the realm of export-control law. A sponsor's desire to limit publication is in conflict with the Fundamental Research Exclusion (FRE) that governs academic research in the United States. A main provision of the FRE is freedom to publish. Therefore, a research sponsor seeking to limit publication in any way moves the project into export-control regulations. This can be a surprise to sponsors and researchers alike, but there are workarounds for such situations that involve executing the project as an export-controlled project.

31. Mervis (2017).

32. Within limits! Institutional policy can impose constraints on how much time faculty devote to consulting, as well as restrict the use of institutional resources for such work (e.g., lab space); institutional intellectual assets can be the subject of carve-out clauses in the consulting agreements.

33. In some cases, faculty chairs or deans or other administrators must review such agreements and approve the consulting arrangement.

34. Individuals are usually prohibited from acting as consultants to any company from which they receive research/service contracts and vice versa.

35. Industry also likes to get free advice from "thought leaders."

36. Novices to nonprofit boards can be surprised to learn that not only are they not paid for their service, but they may be expected to donate to/raise funds for the organization.
37. Nnakwe et al. (2018); NSF (2019).
38. Under Title 15 of US Code §3710a, federal agencies can work with other entities via a Cooperative Research and Development Agreement (CRADA).
39. Federal laboratories are required to pursue commercialization of research results.
40. https://www.nhlbi.nih.gov/grants-and-training/funding-opportunities-and-contacts/NHLBI-Catalyze-Program
41. Crowdfunding is an extension of the decades-old citizen science movement. Many nonprofit organizations enlist volunteers to record information, whether in their back yards (e.g., rainfall, temperature, and the like) or in more structured settings. Perhaps best known is the Audubon Society Christmas bird counts.
42. For example, Steinberg et al. (2012) and Hogue (2015).
43. Graduate students are particularly adept at using such platforms to fund their work (Sauermann et al. 2019).
44. Sauermann et al. (2019).
45. Cotropia (2021) found that products with patents pending are more successful than those already patented.
46. Trying to raise funds as an independent operator outside the university's structure may well violate institutional policy.
47. If the funds are deposited into an institutional account, then the institution has rights to the intellectual assets developed from their use.
48. See launch.umd.edu and crowdfund.vt.edu for two examples.
49. Any company that appears on the TV show *Shark Tank* is likely to attract such investments subsequently.
50. Sauermann et al. (2019) report that women actually see higher returns than men; we return to the topic of investment bias in Chapter 8.
51. Schafer et al. (2018) found that visual appeal and humor in the pitch, as well as postlaunch interactions with the inventor, are predictors of success.
52. While federal laws have been relaxed to allow just about anyone to invest, equity funding platforms in the United States like Wefunder, AngelList, and EquityNet remain subject to oversight by the Securities and Exchange Commission.
53. Big money moving into equity crowdfunding has the potential to push out small investors; however, that does not seem to be happening (Wang et al. 2019).
54. thecrowdfundingcenter.com offers a tool to compare platforms
55. Fundly.com
56. Schafer et al. (2018); Vachelard et al. (2016); Sauermann et al. (2019).
57. Paschen (2017).

PROFILE: Luis von Ahn

1. Check out his TED Talk https://www.ted.com/talks/luis_von_ahn_massive_scale_online_collaboration?language=en
and interview with Guy Roz of NPR https://www.npr.org/2020/05/22/860884062/recaptcha-and-duolingo-luis-von-ahn.

Chapter 6

1. You should be aware of rules governing proposals to agencies that call out marking requirements. Some grant proposals can be "marked" to indicate they contain confidential information, and the confidential information can be excluded from public disclosure. This strategy is more commonly used when funding is sought for efforts already in the commercialization pipeline.
2. When is a disclosure enabling? This is a judgment call, best made by commercialization professionals while you are learning the ropes, and by IP attorneys when any questions exist on matters in various stages of patent development or prosecution.
3. Protection refers to filing for a patent.
4. Bar dates occur in many areas of the law, such as in real estate (foreclosures) and criminal prosecution (statute of limitations).
5. Other obvious ways to avoid an enabling disclosure are to not disclose to outside parties, or to modify any such disclosure by not sharing detailed (enabling) information. For the latter point, preliminary discussions are common with companies that are testing the waters to see if detailed discussions are warranted and, if they are, to move into a CDA/NDA prior to enabling discussions.
6. We have heard many faculty describe a report of invention as a patent filing. Nope.
7. We strongly advise you to be wary about one-sided CDAs in which information shared with you is covered but information you may share is not. In the latter case, your information could be publicly disclosed even if a CDA is in place!
8. CDAs are usually negotiated through the tech transfer or sponsored research offices.
9. Also take into account the actions of your collaborators to ensure they do not disclose!
10. Inventors who repeatedly request last-minute filings to avoid public disclosure cause recurring "fire drill" scrambles. Do not develop a reputation for that behavior!
11. This very broad category includes any tangible materials, including chemical compounds, engineering components, software, supplies, equipment, prototypes, and cell lines.

12. https://ico.sites.stanford.edu/memo-use-mtas
13. https://techtransfer.umich.edu/for-inventors/mta/outgoing. See the decision tree section on this website.
14. NIH convened a meeting in 1990 to establish an efficient process for biological transfers. The resulting product is the UBMTA (Unified Biological Material Transfer Agreement). Parties sign on to the UBMTA terms as an institution by a one-time acceptance of terms. Once parties have signed the agreement (a list of these parties is maintained by the Association of University Technology Managers), transfers with other parties that have also signed this agreement move forward through an implementing letter. The implementing letter documents what is being transferred, payment information, and minimal special terms. No negotiation of terms is required. The UBMTA has a few template options in their MTA toolkit that provide latitude for various materials with specific conditions.
15. Like other agreements, find the party within your institution that handles such matters.
16. https://uidp.org/publication/contract-accord-10-material-transfer-agreements
17. USPTO.gov, WIPO.org, patents.google.com.
18. If an application is filed in the PCT and then at national stage election, it is filed with the United States; the application publishes at 18 months as per PCT provisions. Only if the application is filed solely through the USPTO does it not publish until it issues. There are other circumstances that limit publication, such as a classified patent.
19. You can be scooped by prior art!
20. An inventor has materially contributed to the claims that are actually allowed in the issued patent.
21. The IIA may not be needed immediately. The IIA establishes selection of the lead institution for patent prosecution, marketing, and licensing; it also establishes how patent costs will be shared, and how revenue, if realized, will be apportioned. Typically, the lead inventor's institution becomes the lead on future patent applications. Documenting the contribution allocation up-front allows quick generation of IIAs if they are ever needed. Sometimes putting the IIA in place is not a priority early on, but it can become a fire drill if this remains an outstanding action item at licensing. Analogous to sharing indirect costs on grants, these discussions can become fraught if they occur only when real money is at issue.
22. If your patent application is overreaching, you could block subsequent patent filings with your own art! see also Chapter 4.
23. The design-around step will almost surely be taken by parties potentially interested in licensing a patent or working around the claims in such a patent. Should they uncover approaches to solve the unmet need without your technology, they are unlikely to license your discovery, even if patented.

24. http://keeplearning.engin.umich.edu/intellectual-property/gallery/ 32-designing-around-the-patent-of-another
25. Early assessments are helpful to avoid disasters down the road.
26. If you and your team find this to be the case, please consider design-around exercises based on your deep understanding of the field of research and your experimental efforts thus far. That exercise may point out a new use or embodiment that can be commercialized.
27. Variables to develop the strategy include your history/plans for publication and other public disclosure, relevant funding, plans/commitment to gather more data and information, and preliminary art search information. It is imperative that you work *with* the TTO team to assess the timing options for pursuing a solid patent application. Far too often, inventors want to make these decisions, which are, frankly, out of their expertise domain. If you don't believe that, please re-read Chapter 4. Once the strategy and timing for execution are established, you must live up to your obligations in the plan.
28. In Chapter 4, perspective is offered on the breadth of specifications for the various filing strategies.
29. Marketing can start very early, even before a patent application is filed. In those cases, CDAs will be required for meaningful discussions, but they do not offer protection for your ideas and inventions; a CDA simply prevents public disclosure.
30. Some institutions may not file in the PCT without a licensee; if a licensee is not in place at national stage election, additional filings will likely not be made (see also Chapter 4).
31. Sometimes this happens, but it is rare. No one can champion a technology like the inventor!
32. It also conveys rights to patent applications that are derived from the licensed patent.
33. Keep in mind conflict of interest and conflict of commitment, as we described in Chapter 5.
34. Moving federal grants is subject to approval of both institutions, but industry-sponsored research may not be transferable.
35. Again, subject to negotiation between institutions.
36. And possibly in time your heirs.
37. Including national programs like the Collegiate Inventors Competition, as well as internal funds.

Chapter 7

1. Often misused, the term *entrepreneur* refers to someone who starts a business.
2. Rose and Patterson (2016); Marcolongo (2017); Blank and Dorf (2020); Shimasaki (2020).

3. Aldridge et al. (2017).

4. Indeed, recently graduated students found start-up companies more often than their faculty advisers (Åstebro et al. 2012). They play critical roles in developing the technology for the market (Hayter et al. 2016).

5. A strong idea in the hands of a weak team often fails, whereas a weak idea in the hands of a strong team has a good chance to succeed (especially if they pivot a time or two!).

6. Remember that a start-up company likely must license rights from the institution to develop intellectual assets.

7. White and Burg (2019) analyze this situation in detail.

8. Increasingly, universities are offering special entrepreneurial leaves for faculty who wish to start companies.

9. Beware: in general, faculty do not make good CEOs (Zwilling 2012; Wurmseher 2017).

10. Many folks out there enjoy the start-up environment and move from start-up to start-up as serial entrepreneurs and even serial CEOs.

11. This is actually the norm (Åstebro et al. 2012).

12. This is very difficult for some faculty, and a tendency to micromanage former students can be fatal.

13. A pitch to investors is not a scientific seminar!

14. This term refers to a situation in which you ride an elevator with a potential investor and have six floors to make your case.

15. The VP for some start-ups can be amplified and/or protected by two classes of IP we have not discussed in depth: trademarks and trade secrets (see Chapter 4). These have little relevance to academic researchers, but in a small company they can be critical for brand development and market success.

16. Both of us have started nonprofit organizations.

17. Etkowitz and Leydesdorff (1995); Audretsch et al. (2019).

18. With a caveat: the ecosystem is, for the most part, completely uninterested in lifestyle companies and nonprofits.

19. A notable exception is the Government—University—Industry Research Roundtable (GUIRR) hosted by the National Academies. GUIRR publishes position papers and offers free webinars on a variety of topics focused on the innovation agenda.

20. This is no surprise if you recall the unbaked cake metaphor in Box 7.1. In many instances, to go from raw ingredients to the finished cake is the job of a start-up.

21. See Chapter 5 for discussion of who owns what. Unless the assets were developed entirely without reliance on university sources, a license will be necessary.

22. Express licenses may limit negotiation of terms.

23. A stake in the company, typically taken as shares.

24. An amount as little as $5,000 or any equity could trigger such a policy; be sure you know your institution's policy!

25. Even if the start-up did not derive from institutional assets! These are essentially academic matters, and conflicts policies are usually overseen by deans and/or department chairs rather than the commercialization office.
26. Especially public universities, although this landscape is rapidly changing.
27. Managing grants is not trivial for a small business; to even apply, start-ups must demonstrate readiness, and the actual award terms can be onerous.
28. The International Business Innovation Association (nbia.org) is an umbrella organization.
29. Isabelle (2013) offers a primer on incubators and accelerators.
30. Frequently called spin-out companies.
31. Businesses with 500 or fewer employees.
32. SBIR.gov
33. A federal requirement of STTR grants is that the parties must develop a model rights agreement (and most institutions have such a template) which outlines allocation between the parties of IP rights relating to that project.
34. Principal Investigator/Program Director is the preferred nomenclature for these grants.
35. These grants support research only as it propels business development and should not be viewed as an alternative way to fund basic research (Hayter 2015).
36. There are also Fast Track awards for combined Phase I and II awards.
37. BARDA is playing a key role in propelling new technologies to meet challenges imposed by the SARS-CoV-2 pandemic.
38. Heder (2017).
39. Listed on the SBIR.gov webpage.
40. The frequently described "valley of death" precedes and incorporates the two types of funding (dilutive vs nondilutive); see http://startup-port.com/blog/the-hidden-death-trap-for-all-startups-the-valley-of-death/ and Zwilling (2013).
41. VCs are paid to invest and manage their investors' funds.
42. Such decisions are made after considerable deliberation informed by background work known as due diligence.
43. Dilutive funding can take various forms, from outright issuance of stock to convertible notes leading to issuance of stock and other options.
44. That's why these groups rarely fund lifestyle companies: the expected return on investment is small if the founder never plans to sell.
45. Hundreds of websites outline the components of good pitches to funders.
46. Many large companies have venture funds specifically for investment in start-ups.
47. An example from the COVID-19 pandemic: Merck acquired Themis, a company that had in-licensed vaccine technology from the Pasteur Institute, and Merck had participated on the Themis Board prior to acquisition. In January 2021, Merck announced it would halt its vaccine development efforts, and in March 2021 reported that it would support the COVID-19 vaccine efforts

through the manufacturing and supply of the Jansen/Johnson & Johnson vaccine, with financial support from BARDA to expand manufacturing capacity for vaccines and medicines.

48. Henry et al. (2017).
49. Cbinsights.com
50. But remember there is no free lunch; incubators tie these services to strict accountability criteria, and some require equity in your company.
51. As the products you plan to offer become more solid, you must consider potential infringement of other patents. The most important terms are "clearance search" and "freedom to operate."
52. Wurmseher (2017).

PROFILE: Tish Scolnik

1. A disclaimer: both of us have invested in GRIT; we met Tish when she pitched to our angel consortium.
2. Its priority date of 2009 and issue date of 2014 illustrate the timeline for patents; there are 12 named inventors on this patent, 2 of whom moved into active roles in commercialization of this technology.

Chapter 8

1. There are, of course, numerous accomplished inventors who are women and/or people of color, and we highlight several in our Profiles. Of note in contemporaneous times are Emmanuelle Charpentier and Jennifer Doudna, who were awarded the 2020 Nobel Prize in Chemistry for their groundbreaking work on the new molecular tool CRISPR, which allows targeted gene editing. In addition to their academic research, both of these superstars have patented and founded companies.
2. See, for example, Henry et al. (2017), Poggesi et al. (2020), and Dana (2008).
3. There is a vast literature on this topic. Despite progress over the past 20 years, models predict that reaching gender and ethnic parity will take decades. See, for example, Thomas et al. (2015).
4. Many deride the metaphor of a leaky pipeline, preferring instead to use a maze or hurdle analogy. The consensus is that women remain underrepresented in STEM education and employment. The Society of Women Engineers releases an annual report summarizing the vast literature on this topic (research.swe.org).
5. See the National Science Board's Indicators for a historical snapshot of degree attainment by gender and ethnicity; available at https://nsf.gov/nsb/sei.

6. Corbett and Hill (2015).

7. Civil engineering and biomedical engineering have much higher representation of women than do electrical, mechanical, and aerospace engineering. Computer science has the lowest of any STEM field.

8. Hewitt and Sherbin (2014).

9. Silbert and Dubé (2021).

10. Blume-Kohout (2014).

11. Blume-Kohout (2014) terms this "graduate school imprinting." Interestingly, an exception is mathematics and statistics, in which female graduate students are supported more often than men. Even so, these fields have very low reliance on industry funding, so the impact remains small.

12. Movement from industry to academia is common in engineering, computer science, and some of the biomedical sciences. The On-Ramps program at the University of Washington was designed to facilitate those transitions for women (https://advance.washington.edu/grants/past-initiatives/on-ramps-academia).

13. Thursby and Thursby (2005).

14. Nager et al. (2016) also found that in the United States, foreign-born women patented at a higher rate than native-born.

15. Sugimoto et al. (2015); the USPTO (2019) reviews 40 years of data on inventorship.

16. NASEM (2020a); Henry et al. (2017).

17. Sugimoto et al. (2015).

18. Whittington and Smith-Doerr (2008).

19. The Healthcare Businesswomen's Association (hbanet.org) is a vibrant national organization, with many chapters across the country. This biotech-oriented society offers peer mentoring, professional development seminars, and other venues to promote women's careers in the industry.

20. Joshi et al. (2018); Servo et al. (2020).

21. Nnakwe et al. (2018).

22. For an overview, see Kuschel and Lepeley (2016); the gender gap in incubator space is a global phenomenon (Treanor and Henry 2010; Dahlstrand 2013).

23. Gatewood et al. (2009); Cohoon et al. (2010); Coleman and Robb (2016); Demiralp et al. (2018).

24. California recently enacted a law requiring all firms to have at least one woman on the board, yet compliance has been problematic (Padilla 2020). The global leader for enhancing women's participation on boards is Norway, which requires every board to have at least 40% women.

25. Link and Morrison (2019). These authors examine companies funded by the SBIR program but unfortunately aggregated Asians with other ethnic minorities. Ample data show that success in commercialization by Asian men more closely resembles that of white men than other minorities.

26. Li and Koedel (2017).

27. This is particularly surprising given that the Minority Development Business Agency housed in the Department of Commerce was established in 1969. The Agency does track basic data on minority-owned businesses but research on scientific and technology commercialization by minorities is thin. For example, a recent special issue of the periodical *Small Business Economics* that focuses on minority-owned businesses has but one article with a tech focus.

28. Mervis (2015).

29. Fechner and Shapanka (2018).

30. Jennings and Brush (2013).

31. Stephan and El-Ganainy (2007); Cohoon et al. (2010).

32. Haus et al. (2013); Mueller and Dato-on (2013).

33. Lam (2010); Hoang and Gimeno (2010).

34. Robb et al. (2014); Dalborg et al. (2015).

35. Noguera et al. (2013). Furthermore, our experience strongly indicates that women scientists would far rather take risks in pure research than in commercialization. Thus, familiarity and risk-taking are strongly linked for women.

36. Goel et al. (2015).

37. Network effects are evident throughout multiple pathways to commercialization, from industry funding to angel and venture capital investments.

38. Niehaus and O'Meara (2015).

39. This is the raison d'être for the Healthcare Business Women's Association.

40. Klebanow (1991) provides an early discussion of the complex topic of money and gender.

41. Howe et al. (2014).

42. Bates et al. (2018) review the literature on minority entrepreneurship and focus almost exclusively on demand factors.

43. Dana (2007); Bates et al. (2018).

44. Yao et al. (2005) focus on market investments to gauge risk tolerance. Whether that translates to entrepreneurial risk is unknown.

45. Also called implicit bias. The Nobel-winning economist Daniel Kahneman (2013) includes this effect in his description of "fast thinking." You can test yourself for unconscious biases at implicit.harvard.edu.

46. Aschhoff and Grimpe (2014).

47. Jennings and Brush (2013); Verheul et al. (2012).

48. Stewart and Valian (2018).

49. Servo et al. (2020).

50. O'Meara et al. (2017).

51. Guarino and Borden (2017).

52. Shane et al. (2015) sent fictitious invention disclosures to tech transfer officers and found substantial unconscious bias against women and overt bias against those lacking industry experience.
53. Treanor and Henry (2010).
54. Mervis (2015).
55. Coleman and Robb (2016); Demiralp et al. (2018); Link and Morrison (2019).
56. Blume-Kohout (2014) and Brush et al. (2018); women receive less than 2% of start-up financing, while African American and Latino founders together receive less than 1%.
57. Brooks et al. (2014).
58. Kanze et al. (2018); Brush et al. (2018).
59. *Homophily* plays a large role in investor choice (Hegde and Tumlinson 2014). A great illustration of this concept is the story of SPANX. Founder Sara Blakeley was turned down by (male) investor after (male) investor until she finally was able to model her underwear concept to a female buyer at Neiman Marcus.
60. Bigelow et al. (2012); Reutzel and Belsito (2015).
61. Cook and Kongchaeroen (2010).
62. Especially the Association of American Universities (AAU) and APLU.
63. See Williams-Baron et al. (2018).
64. Howe et al. (2014). One important lesson from this program is that women become interested in commercialization when it is framed as a vehicle for societal impact.
65. Mercier et al. (2018).
66. Sexton and Ligler (2018).
67. Notably, the American Association for the Advancement of Science (AAAS) Invention Ambassador program (Comedy and Dougherty 2018); AUTM has a committee focused on encouraging women inventors.
68. Cantwell (2014); Gafni et al. (2021); Bapna and Ganco (2020).
69. Gafni et al. (2021).
70. See Coleman and Robb (2016) and Sposato (2017).
71. Wallace and Conti (2015) give a brief history of Golden Seeds and affiliated angel groups; they tend to be founded by women and thus typify what Greenberg and Mollick (2017) call activist choice homophily. While men constitute a growing percentage of these gender-biased angel groups, they are dominated by women investors.
72. About 80% of Golden Seeds members are women.
73. Blume-Kohout (2014).
74. See https://www.entrepreneur.com/article/282529 and https://startupnation.com/start-your-business/small-business-grants-women-minorities/
75. https://www.kauffman.org/currents/inclusion-open-inclusive-entrepreneurship-funding

PROFILE: Pingsha Dong

1. A not-for-profit research and development giant and U.S. government contractor managing and co-managing numerous national labs. DISCLOSURE: JES was working at Battelle at the same time.
2. Including JES!
3. US 6,901,809 priority date in 2000 issued in 2005 was the first, and others have followed.

Chapter 9

1. Swamidass (2013).
2. AUTM (2018).
3. AUTM (2018); there are numerous reasons why a patent application might not issue. For example, claims might be disallowed, or the application may be abandoned.
4. Wisnioski and Vinsel (2019); Marcus (2021).

PROFILE: Commercialization in the U.S. Department of Agriculture

1. This is its value proposition!

Epilogue: Messages to Administrators and Commercialization Staff

1. Other components of the rewards system include salaries, lab space, teaching and service assignments, and the like; they have relatively little bearing on effective tech transfer.
2. See APLU (2015) and NASEM (2020a)
3. We certainly do not suggest that these be mandatory, only that they be included.
4. We also know that the department chair has a strong influence on faculty's involvement with commercialization (Greven et al. 2019).
5. Cassuto and Weisbuch (2021).
6. Beyhan and Findik (2018).
7. Åstebro et al. (2012).
8. We are sure that your institution does this, as stories in newsletters and on webpages as well as posts in social media. Here we are suggesting that it become formalized within review procedures.

9. The IP policy can include this point, providing details on allocation of square footage, proportion of effort, and use of equipment, among others.

10. DeVol et al. (2017).

11. The T2 PlayBook (https://federallabs.org/t2-toolkit/t2-playbook) is a marvelous compilation of best practices.

12. Especially because your institution is on the hook for patent costs until a license deal is signed.

13. By contrast, the federal lab systems and other research organizations have tech transfer baked into their cultures.

14. In our experience, faculty rarely ask what your technical words and phrases mean, so be sure to explain when you must use a term like *public disclosure* or *bar date*. And recognize that faculty believe when they submit the report of invention to your office, they are protected; some even think they have a patent.

15. Indeed, such discussions bring depth to the team responsible for any particular technology, and they also provide backup in case life happens to you.

16. Fire sales can be effective! If your office is thinking about discontinuing support of a particular technology, alerting potential licensees that it might be inexpensively licensed can be sufficient to close a deal. This issue is delicate, of course, but one last try before the invention moves into the public domain can pay off.

17. For our international readers: "There is no I in team" expresses the view that the individual's wants and needs must be secondary to the group's.

Glossary

accelerator/boot camp a training program to help start-ups grow and develop

angel an individual who invests personal funds in start-ups

assignee individual or entity that owns an asset

bar date in patent law, the date after which no patent application can be filed

business plan detailed plans for achieving financial and operational goals for a business (including revenues and expenses)

claims (issued) specific subject matter protected in an issued patent

conflict of commitment situation in which outside activities interfere with obligations to primary employer

conflict of interest circumstances in which actions for a primary interest (e.g., research activities) are influenced by a secondary interest (career or financial gains)

copyright a form of intellectual property protection for written documents, works of art, and other intellectual assets that have been reduced to a medium of expression

crowdfunding a virtual platform to attract/invest funds from interested parties anywhere in the world

deliverables specific items that must be provided per a legally binding agreement

dilutive/nondilutive funding investment that requires a share of company ownership (dilutive)/investment not requiring partial ownership of the company (nondilutive)

elect title (under Bayh-Dole) action taken by a federal contractor to obtain ownership of an invention

embodiment description of how an invention can be used, made, practiced

enabling public disclosure communication to a third party in sufficient detail to practice an invention

encumbrance grant of rights held by a party

enforcement period time left in patent term after issuance

entrepreneur someone who starts a business

equity ownership in a company, usually in the form of shares

exclusive licensee the only entity that can utilize via an exclusive license agreement the patent or asset rights conveyed via license agreement

exercise the option action taken by an optionee to initiate negotiations for a license

exit sale or other disposition of a business entity

export controls regulations set by the federal government concerning export of goods and technology

grant of rights conveyance of rights in and to specific intellectual assets being transferred in a legally binding agreement

incubator a location that houses start-up companies

infringement violation of exclusive rights granted in a patent

intellectual assets broad definition including intellectual property and other tangible assets such as proprietary materials and data

intellectual property patent applications, patents, copyrighted items, trade secrets, trade dress, and trademarks

intentional investing investments that seek to counteract bias

invalidation (of patents) successful outcome of a legal challenge to an issued patent

invention report documentation of a discovery, insight, or technology supplied to the TTO; also referred to as invention disclosure, report of invention, or intellectual property disclosure report; *not a patent application!*

license legally binding agreement conveying rights to intellectual assets and related specified matter

lifestyle company business that (originally) does not seek investment requiring exit

market pull market need drives innovation and market adoption

national stage election selection of PCT countries for individual patent filings

office action written prosecution correspondence from a patent examiner that must be answered within a specified timeframe

option agreement legally binding agreement typically conveying short-term non-commercial grant of rights to intellectual assets

patent grant of rights by a government allowing exclusive rights to make, use, sell, offer to sell, and import the subject matter in the claims

patent issue date date when a patent office issues a patent following allowance and payment of issuance fee

patent prosecution filing of a patent application and correspondence/exchanges between the patent office and the applicant concerning claims allowability

patent term length of time from date of first filing

pivot change of business focus, often in a start-up company platform technology innovation that can be used for multiple applications or markets

prior art information publicly available prior to a patent first filing, used to assess novelty and nonobviousness for patent claims

priority date date of first filing of a patent application

provisional patent application placeholder patent filing that establishes a priority date

public disclosure unprotected discussion with a third party

public domain available to the public with no encumbrance

reduced to practice demonstrated practical utility of an invention or idea

royalty percentage of net sales payment from licensee to licensor

SARS-CoV-2 the virus that causes COVID-19

search report written communication from a patent office providing references to prior art for use in assessing claims patentability

specification all matter in the patent application or patent other than the abstract and claims

start-up company business founded to develop a product/service for a market; academic start-ups are sometimes called spin-outs

technology push innovation without a clear market

term duration of a legally binding agreement

term sheet exhibit on an option agreement providing selected financial parameters for a subsequent license agreement should the option be exercised

trade dress characteristics of the visual appearance of a product, its packaging, or a structure that signify the source of the product to consumers

trade secret form of intellectual property that is confidential information not generally known or readily ascertained by others; has economic value if protected from public disclosure and may be sold or licensed. Trade secrets are prohibited in federally-funded research.

trademark an indicator of the source of products or services, such as a word(s), sign, design, expression, color, or sound, which identifies products or services of a particular source from those of others; a form of intellectual property

unconscious bias unintended mental associations that devalue the abilities or traits of individuals from some groups

use/licensed use market applications or field(s) for which a grant of rights is given

value proposition description of foundational product/service a company offers, which differentiates it from other competitor products/services on the market

venture capital private equity financing provided to start-ups and rigorously managed

References

Aldridge, T. T., D. B. Audretsch, S. Desai, and V. Nadella. 2017. Scientist entrepreneurship across scientific fields. In *Universities and the Entrepreneurial Ecosystem*, edited by D. B. Audretsch and A. N. Link, 67–84. Northampton, MA: Edward Elgar.

Andersen, J. P., M. W. Nielson, N. L. Simone, R. E. Lewiss, and R. Jagsi. 2020. Meta-research: COVID-19 medical papers have fewer women first authors than expected. *eLife*9: e58807.

APLU. 2015. *APLU Task Force on Tenure, Promotion and Technology Transfer. Survey Results and Next Steps*. Washington, DC.

Aschhoff, B., and C. Grimpe. 2014. Contemporaneous peer effects, career age, and the industry involvement of academics in biotechnology. *Research Policy* 43: 367–381.

Åstebro, T., N. Bazzazian, and S. Braguinsky. 2012. Startups by recent university graduates and their faculty: Implications for university entrepreneurship policy. *Research Policy* 41: 663–677.

Audretsch, D. B., J. A. Cunningham, D. F. Kuratko, E. E. Lehmann, and M. Menter. 2019. Entrepreneurial ecosystems: Economic, technological, and societal impacts. *Journal of Technology Transfer* 44: 313–325.

Audretsch, D. B., and A. N. Link. 2017. *Universities and the Entrepreneurial Ecosystem*. Northampton, MA: Edward Elgar.

AUTM. 2018. *AUTM 2018 Licensing Activity Survey*. Association of University Technology Managers, Chicago IL.

Bapna, S., and M. Ganco. 2020. Gender gaps in equity crowdfunding: Evidence from a randomized field experiment. *Management Science* Articles in Advance: 1–32.

Bates, T., W. D. Bradford, and R. Seamans. 2018. Minority entrepreneurship in twenty-first century America. *Small Business Economics* 50: 415–427.

Bergman, A. B. 1986. Academic hubris. *Pediatrics* 77: 251–256.

Beyhan, B., and D. Findik. 2018. Student and graduate entrepreneurship: Ambidextrous universities create more nascent entrepreneurs. *Journal of Technology Transfer* 43: 1346–1374.

Bigelow, L., L. Lundmark, J. M. Parks, and R. Wuebker. 2012. Skirting the issues: Experimental evidence of gender bias in IPO prospectus evaluations. *Journal of Management* 40: 1732–1759.

Biomedical Research Workforce Working Group. 2012. *Report*. National Institutes of Health, Bethesda MD.

Blank, S., and B. Dorf. 2020. *The Startup Owner's Manual*. Hoboken, NJ: Wiley.

Blume-Kohout, M. E. 2014. *Understanding the Gender Gap in STEM Fields Entrepreneurship*. U.S. Small Business Administration, Washington DC.

Brooks, A. W., L. Huang, S. W. Kearney, and F. E. Murray. 2014. Investors prefer entrepreneurial ventures pitched by attractive men. *Proceedings of the National Academy of Sciences USA* 111: 4427–4431.

Brush, C. G., P. G. Greene, L. Balachandra, and A. Davis. 2018. The gender gap in venture capital—progress, problems, and perspectives. *Venture Capital* 20: 115–136.

Buenstorf, G. 2009. Is commercialization good or bad for science? Individual-level evidence from the Max Planck Society. *Research Policy* 38: 281–292.

Campbell, C. M., and K. O'Meara. 2014. Faculty agency: Departmental contexts that matter in faculty careers. *Research in Higher Education* 55: 49–74.

Cantwell, M. 2014. *21st Century Barriers to Women's Entrepreneurship. Majority Report of the US Senate Committee on Small Business and Entrepreneurship.* United States Senate, Washington, DC.

Cassuto, L., and R. A. Weisbuch. 2021. *The New PhD: How to Build a Better Graduate Education*. Baltimore, MD: Johns Hopkins University Press.

Chisum, D. S. 1997. *Chisum on Patents*. Newark, NJ: Matthew Bender and Co.

Cleary, G. E., J. M. Beierlein, N. S. Khanuja, L. M. McNamee, and F. D. Ledley. 2018. Contribution of NIH funding to new drug approvals 2010–2016. *Proceedings of the National Academy of Sciences USA* 115: 2329–2334.

Cohoon, J. M., V. Wadhwa, and L. Mitchell. 2010. *The Anatomy of an Entrepreneur: Are Successful Women Entrepreneurs Different from Men?* Ewing Marion Kauffman Foundation, Kansas City, MO.

Coleman, S., and A. M. Robb. 2016. *The Next Wave: Financing Women's Growth-oriented Firms*. Stanford, CA: Stanford University Press.

Comedy, Y. L., and E. L. Dougherty. 2018. Breaking barriers: Female inventors blazing a path forward. *Technology and Innovation* 19: 751–758.

Cook, L. D., and C. Kongcharoeon. 2010. *The Idea Gap in Pink and Black*. National Bureau of Economic Research, Cambridge, MA.

Corbett, C., and C. Hill. 2015. *Solving the Equation: the Variables for Women's Success in Engineering and Computing.* American Association of University Women, Washington, DC.

Cotropia, C. A. 2021. Patents as signal of quality in crowdfunding. *University of Illinois Law Review*, 2021: 193–227.

Dahlstrand, Å. L. 2013. Women business ventures in Swedish university incubators. *International Journal of Gender and Entrepreneurship* 5: 78–96.

Dalborg, C., Y. von Friedrichs, and J. Wincent. 2015. Risk perception matters: Why women's passion may not lead to a business start-up. *International Journal of Gender and Entrepreneurship* 7: 87–104.

Dana, L. P. 2008. *Handbook of Research on Ethnic Minority Entrepreneurship: A Co-evolutionary View on Resource Management*. Northampton, MA: Edward Elgar Publishing.

Demiralp, B., L. T. R. Morrison, and S. Zayed. 2018. On the commercialization path: entrepreneurship and intellectual property outputs among women in STEM. *Technology and Innovation* 19: 707–726.

Deryugina, T., O. Shuchkov, and J. E. Stearns. 2021. *COVID-19 disruptions dispro-portionately affect female academics.* National Bureau of Economic Research, Cambridge, MA.

DeVol, R., J. Lee, and M. Ratnatunga. 2017. *Concept to Commercialization: The Best Universities for Technology Transfer.* Milken Institute, Washington, DC.

Diamandis, E., and N. Bouras. 2018. Hubris and Sciences. *F1000 Research* 7: 133.

Etkowitz, H., and L. Leydesdorff. 1995. The triple helix—University–Industry–Government relations: A laboratory for knowledge based economic development. *EASST Review* 14: 14–19.

Fanelli, D. 2010. "Positive" results increase down the hierarchy of the sciences. *PLoS One* 5: e10068.

Fechner, H., and M. S. Shapanka. 2018. Closing diversity gaps in innovation: Gender, race, and income disparities in patenting and commercialization of inventions. *Technology and Innovation* 19: 727–734.

Fulweiler, R. W., S. W. Davies, J. F. Biddle, A. J. Burgin, E. H. G. Cooperdock, T. C. Hanley, et al. 2021. Rebuild the academy: Supporting academic mother during COVID-19 and beyond. *PLoS Biology* 19: e3001100.

Gafni, H., D. Marom, A. Robb, and O. Sade. 2021. Gender dynamics in crowd-funding (Kickstarter): Evidence on entrepreneurs, investors, deals, and taste-based discrimination. *Review of Finance* 25: 235–274.

Gatewood, E. J., C. G. Brush, N. M. Carter, P. G. Greene, and M. M. Hart. 2009. Diana: A symbol of women entrepreneurs' hunt for knowledge, money, and the rewards of entrepreneurship. *Small Business Economics* 32: 129–144.

Genschaft, J., J. Wickert, B. Gray-Little, K. Hanson, R. B. Marchase, P. E. Schiffer, and R. M. Tanner. 2016. Consideration of technology transfer in tenure and pro-motion. *Technology and Innovation* 17: 197–204.

Goel, R. K., D. Göktepe-Hultén, and R. Ram. 2015. Academics' entrepreneurship propensities and gender differences. *Journal of Technology Transfer* 40: 161–177.

Gores, T., and A. N. Link. 2021. The globalization of the Bayh-Dole act. *Annals of Science and Technology Policy* 5: 1–90.

Gouldin, C., and C. Rouse. 2000. Orchestrating impartiality: The impact of "blind" auditions on female musicians. *American Economic Review* 90: 715–741.

Greenberg, J., and E. Mollick. 2017. Activist choice homophily and the crowd-funding of female founders. *Administrative Science Quarterly* 62: 341–374.

Greven, A., S. Strese, and M. Brettel. 2020. Determining scientists' academic en-gagement: Perception of academic chairs' entrepreneurial orientation and net-work capablitiies. *Journal of Technology Transfer* 45: 1376–1404.

Gruber, J., and S. Johnson. 2019. *Jump-starting America: How Breakthrough Science Can Revive Economic Growth and the American Dream.* New York: Public Affairs.

Guarino, C. M., and V. M. H. Borden. 2017. Faculty service loads and gender: Are women taking care of the academic family? *Research in Higher Education* 58: 672–694.

Guerzoni, N., T. T. Aldridge, D. B. Audretsch, and S. Desai. 2014. A new industry creation and originality: Insight from the funding sources of university patents. *Research Policy* 43: 1697–1706.

Hardré, P. L., and S. Kollmann. 2012. Motivational implications of faculty performance standards. *Educational Management Administration and Leadership* 40: 724–751.

Haus, I., H. Steinmetz, R. Isidor, and R. Kabst. 2013. Gender effects on entrepreneurial intention: A meta-analytical structural equation model. *International Journal of Gender and Entrepreneurship* 5: 130–156.

Hayter, C. S. 2015. Public or private entrepreneurship? Revisiting motivations and definitions of success among academic entrepreneurs. *Journal of Technology Transfer* 40: 1003–1015.

Hayter, C. S., R. Lubnynsky, and S. Maroulis. 2016. Who is the academic entrepreneur? The role of graduate students in the development of university spinoffs. *Journal of Technology Transfer* 42: 1237–1254.

Heder, M. 2017. From NASA to EU: The evolution of the TRL scale in public sector innovation. *The Innovation Journal: The Public Sector Innovation Journal* 22: article 3.

Hegde, D., and K. Tumlinson. 2014. Does social proximity enhance business partnerships? Theory and evidence from ethnicity's role in US venture capital. *Management Science* 60: 2355–2380.

Henry, C., T. Nelson, and K. Lewis. 2017. *Routledge Companion to Global Female Entrepreneurship.Routledge Companions in Business, Management and Accounting.* New York: Routledge.

Hewitt, S. A., and L. Sherbin. 2014. *Athena Factor 2.0: Accelerating Female Talent in Science, Engineering and Technology.* Center for Talent Innovation, New York.

Higginbotham, E., and M. L. Dahlberg (eds.). 2021. *The Impact of COVID-19 on the Careers of Women in Sciences, Engineering, and Medicine.* National Academy of Sciences, Engineering, and Medicine, Washington, DC.

Hoang, H. A., and J. Gimeno. 2010. Becoming a founder: How founder role identity affects entrepreneurial transitions and persistance in founding. *Journal of Business Venturing* 25: 41–53.

Hockaday, T. 2020. *Technology Transfer: What It's about and How to Do It.* Baltimore, MD: Johns Hopkins University Press.

Hogue, J. 2015. *Step by Step Crowdfunding: Everything You Need to Raise Money from the Crowd.* New York: Efficient Alpha.

Howe, S. A., M. C. Juhas, and J. M. Herbers. 2014. Academic women: Overlooked entrepreneurs. *Peer Review* 16: 17–20.

Isabelle, D. A. 2013. Key factors affecting a techology entrepreneur's choice of incubator or accelerator. *Technology Innovation Management Review* 3: 16–22.

Jennings, J. E., and C. G. Brush. 2013. Research on women entrepreneurs. *The Academy of Management Annals* 7: 661–713.

Johnson, D. R. 2017. *A Fractured Profession: Commercialism and Conflict in Academic Science.* Baltimore, MD: Johns Hopkins University Press.

Joshi, A. M., T. M. Inouye, and J. A. Robinson. 2018. How does agency workforce diversity influence federal R&D funding of minority and women technology entrepreneurs? An analysis of the SBIR and STTR programs, 2001–2011. *Small Business Economics* 50: 499–519.

Kahneman, D. 2013. *Thinking, Fast and Slow.* New York: Farrar, Straus and Giroux.

Kanze, D., L. Huang, M. A. Conley, and Higgins E. T. 2018. We ask men to win and women not to lose: Closing the gender gap in startup funding. *Academy of Management Journal* 61: 586–614.

Key, S. 2017. In today's market, do patents even matter? *Forbes,* November 13.

Khor, E. 2014. *From Academia to Entrepreneur: Lessons from the Real World.* New York: Academic Press.

Kirchberger, M. A., and L. Pohl. 2016. Technology commercialization: A literature review of success factors and antecedents across different contexts. *Journal of Technology Transfer* 41: 1077–1112.

Klebanow, S. 1991. Power, gender, and money. In *Money and Mind,* edited by S. Klebanow and E. L. Lowenkopf, 55–59. Boston, MA: Springer.

Kramer, J. 2020. Women in science may suffer lasting career damage from COVID-19. *Scientific American,* August 12. Accessed at https://www.scientificameri can.com/article/women-in-science-may-suffer-lasting-career-damage-from-covid-19/.

Kuschel, K., and M. T. Lepeley. 2016. Women start-ups in technology: Literature review and research agenda to improve participation. *International Journal of Entrepreneurial Behavior and Research* 27: 333–346.

Lam, A. 2010. From "ivory tower traditionalists" to "entrepreneurial scientists": Academic scientists in fuzzy university-industry boundaries. *Social Studies of Science* 40: 307–340.

Laursen, S., and A. E. Austin. 2020. *Building Gender Equity in the Academy: Institutional Strategies for Change.* Baltimore, MD: Johns Hopkins University Press.

Li, D., and C. Koedel. 2017. Representation and salary gaps by race-ethnicity and gender at selective public universities. *Educational Researcher* 46: 343–354.

Link, A. N. and L. T. R. Morrison. 2019. *Innovative Activity in Minority-owned and Women-owned Business: Evidence from the U.S. Small Business Innovation Research Program.* New York: Springer.

Link, A. N., and J. T. Scott. 2019. The economic benefits of technology transfer from U.S. federal laboratories. *Journal of Technology Transfer* 44: 1416–1426.

Marcolongo, M. 2017. *Academic entrepreneurship : How to Bring Your Scientific Discovery to a Successful Commercial Product.* Hoboken, NJ: Wiley.

Marcus, J. 2020. Think universities are making lots of money from inventions? Think again. *Washington Post,* January 17. Accessed at https://www.washingtonp ost.com/local/education/think-universities-are-making-lots-of-money-from-inventions-think-again/2020/01/16/3989e448-362f-11ea-bb7b-265f4554af6d_ story.html.

Mason, M. A., N. H. Wolfinger, and M. Goulden. 2013. *Do Babies Matter? Gender and Family in the Ivory Tower.* Rutgers, NJ: Rutgers University Press.

Mercier, N. R., V. Ranjit, and R. J. Reardon. 2018. Engaging women innovators: Analytical support for women innovator programming in university technology transfer. *Technology and Innovation* 19: 685–699.

Mervis, J. 2015. NIH program fails to launch blacks in biotech. *Science* 350: 896.

Mervis, H. 2017. Data check: Federal share of basic research hits new low. *Science* 355: 1005.

Michelson, E. S. 2020. *Philanthropy and the Future of Science and Technology*. New York: Routledge.

Mireles, M. E. 2006. States as innovation systems laboratories. *Cardozo Law Review* 2006–2007: 1133–1178.

Misra, J., D. Clark, and E. L. Mickey. 2021. Keeping COVID-19 from sidelining equity. *Inside Higher Ed*, February 10. Accessed at https://www.insidehighered.com/views/2021/02/10/without-intentional-interventions-pandemic-will-make-higher-education-less-diverse.

Moss-Racusin, C. A., J. F. Dovidio, V. L. Brescoll, M. J. Graham, and J. Handelsman. 2012. Science faculty's subtle gender biases favor male students. *Proceedings of the National Academy of Sciences USA* 109: 16474–16479.

Mueller, S. L., and M. C. Dato-on. 2013. A cross cultural study of gender-role orientation and entrepreneurial self-efficacy. *International Entrepreneurship and Management Journal* 9: 1–20.

Myers, K. R., W. Y. Tham, Y. Yin, N. Cohodes, J. G. Thursby, J. C. Thursby, et al. 2020. Unequal effects of the COVID-19 pandemic on scientists. *Nature Human Behavior* 4: 880–883.

Nager, A., D. Hart, S. Ezell, and R. D. Atkinson. 2016. *The Demographics of Innovation in the United States*. Information Technology and Innovation Foundation, Washington, DC.

NASEM. 2019. *Adapting to the 21st Century Innovation Environment*. National Academies of Sciences, Engineering and Medicine, Washington, DC.

NASEM. 2020a. *Promising Practices for Addressing the Underrepresentation of Women in Science, Engineering, and Medicine: Opening Doors*. National Academies of Sciences, Engineering, and Medicine, Washington, DC.

NASEM. 2020b. *Re-envisioning Promotion and Advancement for STEM Faculty: Proceedings of a Workshop in Brief*. National Academies of Sciences, Engineering, and Medicine, Washington, DC.

Niehaus, E., and K. O'Meara. 2015. Invisible but essential: The role of professional networks in promoting faculty agency in career advancement. *Innovative Higher Education* 40: 159–171.

Nnakwe, C. C., N. Cooch, and A. Huang-Saad. 2018. Investing in academic technology innovation and entrepreneurship: Moving beyond research funding through the NSF I-CORPS Program. *Technology and Innovation* 19: 773–7886.

Noguera, M., C. Alvarez, and D. Urbano. 2013. Socio-cultural factors and female entrepreneurship. *International Entrepreneurship and Management Journal* 9: 183–197.

NSF. 2019. *National Science Foundation Innovation Corps (I-CORPS™)*. National Science Foundation, Alexandria, VA.

O'Meara, K., A. Kuvaeva, G. Nyunt, C. Waugaman, and R. Jackson. 2017. Asked more often: Gender differences in faculty workload in research universities and the work interactions that shape them. *American Educational Research Journal* 54: 1154–1186.

Padilla, A. 2020. *Women on Boards*. State of California, Sacramento, CA.

Paschen, J. 2017. Choose wisely: Crowdfunding through the stages of the startup life cycle. *Business Horizons* 60: 179–188.

Perkmann, M., R. Salandra, V. Tartari, M. McKelvey, and A. Hughes. 2021. Academic engagement: A review of the literature 2011–2019. *Research Policy* 50: 104114.

Poggesi, S., M. Mari, L. De Vita, and L. Foss. 2020. Women entrepreneurship in STEM fields: Literature review and future research avenues. *International Entrepreneurship and Management Journal* 16: 17–41.

Reutzel, C. R., and C. A. Belsito. 2015. Female directors and IPO underpricing in the US. *International Journal of Gender and Entrepreneurship* 7: 27–44.

Roach, M., and H. Sauermann. 2010. A taste for science? PhD scientists' academic orientation and self-selection into research careers in industry. *Research Policy* 39: 422–434.

Robb, A. M., S. Coleman, and D. Stangler. 2014. *Sources of Economic Hope: Women's Entrepreneurship*. Ewing Marion Kauffman Foundation, Kansas City, Mo.

Roberts, R. M. 1989. *Serendipity: Accidental Discoveries in Science*. New York: Wiley.

Rose, D., and C. Patterson. 2016. *Research to Revenue*. Chapel Hill, NC: University of North Carolina Press.

Sanberg, P. R., M. Gharib, P. T. Harker, E.W. Kaler, R. B. Marchase, T. D. Sands, et al. 2014. Changing the academic culture: Valuing patents and commercialization toward tenure and career advancement. *Proceedings of the National Academy of Sciences USA* 111: 6542–6547.

Sauermann, H., C. Franzoni, and K. Shafi. 2019. Crowdfunding scientific research: Descriptive insights and correlates of funding success. *PLoS one* 14: e0208384.

Schafer, M. S., J. Metag, J. Feustle, and L. Herzog. 2018. Selling science 2.0: What scientific projects receive crowdfunding online? *Public Understanding of Science* 27: 496–514.

Servo, J. C., V. S. Verostek, K. Lidoro, D. Meane, K. Johnson, and T. Pipher. 2020. *Women's Inclusion in Small Business Innovation Research and Small Business Technology Transfer Programs*. National Women's Business Council, Washington, DC.

Sexton, K. B., and F.S. Ligler. 2018. Strategies to close the gender gap in invention and technology commercialization. *Technology and Innovation* 19: 701–706.

Shane, S., S. A. M. Dolmanas, J. Jankowski, I. M. M. J. Reymen, and G. L. Romme. 2015. Academic entrepreneurship: Which inventors do technology licensing officers prefer for spinoffs? *Journal of Technology Transfer* 40: 273–292.

Sharma, A., A. Jacob, M. Tandon, and D. Kumar. 2010. Orphan drug: Development trends and strategies. *Journal of Pharmacy and Bioallied Sciences* 2: 290–299.

Shimasaki, C., ed. 2020. *Biotechnology Entrepreneurship*. 2nd ed. New York Academic Press.

Silbert, A., and C. M. Dubé. 2021. *The power gap among top earners at America's elite universities*. EOS Foundation, Harwich Port, MA.

Singer, P. L. 2014. *Advances that Stem from Federal Research Support*. The Information Technology and Innovation Foundation, Washington, DC.

Skloot, R. 2010. *The Immortal Life of Henrietta Lacks*. New York: Crown Publishers.

Sposato, J. 2017. *Working Together: 8 Ways Working with Women Leads to Extraordinary Products and Profits*. Hoboken NJ: Wiley-Blackwell.

Steinberg, S., R. Demaria, J. Kimmich, and E. Migicovsky. 2012. *The Crowdfunding Bible: How to Raise Money for Any Startup, Video Game, or Project*. lulu.com.

Stenard, B. S., and H. Sauermann. 2016. Educational mismatch, work outcomes, and entry into entrepreneurship. *Organization Science* 27: 801–824.

Stephan, P. E., and A. El-Ganainy. 2007. The entrepreneurial puzzle: Explaining the gender gap. *Journal of Technology Transfer* 32: 475–487.

Stevens, S. 2004. The enactment of Bayh-Dole. *Journal of Technology Transfer* 29: 93–99.

Stewart, A. J., and V. Valian. 2018. *An Inclusive Academy: Achieving Diversity and Excellence*. Cambridge, MA: MIT Press.

Sugimoto, C. R., C. Ni, J. D. West, and V. Larivière. 2015. The academic advantage: Gender disparities in patenting. *PLoS one* 10: e0128000.

Swamidass, P. M. 2013. University startups as a commercialization alternative: Lessons from three contrasting case studies. *Journal of Technology Transfer* 38: 788–808.

Thomas, N. R., D. J. Poole, and J. M. Herbers. 2015. Gender in science and engineering faculties: Demographic inertia revisited. *PLoS one* 10: e0139767.

Thursby, J. G., and M. C. Thursby. 2005. Gender patterns of research and licensing activity of science and engineering faculty. *Journal of Technology Transfer* 30: 343–353.

Treanor, L., and C. Henry. 2010. Gender in campus incubation: Evidence from Ireland. *International Journal of Gender and Entrepreneurship* 2: 130–149.

USPTO. 2019. *Progress and Potential: A Profile of Women Inventors on U.S. Patents*. United States Patent and Trademark Office, Alexandria, VA.

Vachelard, J, T. Gambarra-Soares, G. Augustini, P. Riul, and V. Maracaja-Coutinho. 2016. A guide to scientific crowdfunding. *PLoS Biology* 14: e1002373.

Verheul, I., R. Thunk, I. Grilo, and P. van der Zwan. 2012. Explaining preferences and actual involvement in self-employment: Gender and the entrepreneurial personality. *Journal of Economic Psychology* 33: 325–341.

Wallace, P., and R. Conti. 2015. Women angel investors. In *Angels without Borders*, edited by J. May and M. M. Liu, 25–31. Singapore: World Scientific Publishing.

Wang, W., A. Mahmood, C. Sismeiro, and N. Vulkan. 2019. The evolution of equity crowdfunding: Insights from co-investments of angels and the crowd. *Research Policy* 48: 103727.

White, N., and K. Burg. 2019. From university to invention to entrepreneurship. *Technology and Innovation* 20: 377–383.

Whittington, K. B., and L. Smith-Doerr. 2008. Women inventors in context: Disparities in patenting across academia and industry. *Gender and Society* 22: 194–218.

Williams-Baron, E., J. Milli, and B. Gault. 2018. *Innovation and Intellectual Property among Women Entrepreneurs*. Institute for Women's Policy Research, Washington, DC.

Wilson, M. A. 2019. Crowdfunding science. *Genome Biology* **20**: 250.

Wisnioski, M., and L. Vinsel. 2019. The campus innovation myth. *Chronicle of Higher Education*, June 11. Accessed at https://www.chronicle.com/article/the-campus-innovation-myth/.

Witteman, H. O., J. Haverfield, and C. Tannenbaum. 2021. COVID-19 gender policy changes support female scientists and improve research quality. *Proceedings of the National Academy of Sciences USA* 118: e2023476118.

Wurmseher, M. 2017. To each his own: Matching different entrepreneurial models to the academic scientists' individual needs. *Technovation* 59: 1–17.

Yao, R., M. S. Gutter, and S. D. Hanna. 2005. The financial risk tolerance of blacks, Hispanics, and whites. *Journal of Financial Counseling and Planning* 16: 51–62.

Zwilling, M. 2012. Inventor-entrepreneur pairs are ideal for a startup. *Forbes*, May 3. Accessed at https://www.forbes.com/sites/martinzwilling/2012/05/02/inventor-entrepreneur-pairs-are-ideal-for-a-startup/?sh=33430d411197

Zwilling, M. 2013. 10 ways for startups to survive the valley of death. *Forbes*, February 18. Accessed at https://www.forbes.com/sites/martinzwilling/2013/02/18/10-ways-for-startups-to-survive-the-valley-of-death/?sh=c4699f169eff.

Index